Welcome to
Pat Doran's

Phonics Steps to Reading Success

A Fast-paced, Word-attack System
For Developing & Improving
Reading Skills

4th Edition
_____

Pat Doran's

Phonics Steps to Reading Success

A Fast-paced, Word-attack System For Developing & Improving Reading Skills

4th Edition

Pat Doran, M.Ed.

Contributors
Lisa Cragg,
Joy Doran,
with
Theresa Manriquez, M.Ed.

978-0-9771101-4-8   Pat Doran's *Phonics Steps to Reading Success: A Fast-Paced, Word-Attack System for Developing and Improving Reading Skills* [PSRS], 4th Ed.
Full-color for Instruction or Self-Study

- Word-for-word phonics lessons on 4 audio CD's optional
- For teachers, parents, and for individual use for self-study
- **Full color** with spiral binding. (Color cues used as instructional strategies.)
- Includes user-friendly scripted instruction on each page and extra Page-by-Page Helpful Hints to aid the new or experienced instructor
- Includes a reproducible spelling journal and phonics rules aligned with PSRS.

SUGGESTED USE: For one-to-one tutoring.
For independent study or literacy centers when used with audio.
For large-group instruction when used on document projector taught.
(Optional: Provide black-and-white Student Version for each student. See below.)

978-0-9771101-3-1   Pat Doran's *Phonics Steps to Reading Success: A Fast-Paced, Word-Attack System for Developing and Improving Reading Skills* [PSRS], 4th Ed.
Black-and-white Student Version

- Black and white with perfect-bound [typical paperback spine] binding.
- Includes scripted instruction on each page and extra Page-by-Page Helpful Hints to aid the new or experienced instructor.
- Can be used alone for instruction, but less effective without color coding.
- Is effective as a support book when used with full-color version.
- Includes spelling and vocabulary journals plus phonics rules aligned with PSRS pages,

SUGGESTED USE: For individual tutoring, for class work/practice and review, independent study/review in class, homework, individual phonics and vocabulary study, and learning centers.

978-0-9771101-6-2   Pat Doran's *Phonics Steps to Reading Success: A Fast-Paced, Word-Attack System for Developing and Improving Reading Skills* [PSRS], 4th Ed.
Large, Class/Group Study Cards

- Approximately 8 ½" x 11" for classroom study and word walls.
- Full Color, glossy card stock
- Includes consonant sounds' chart, phonics concepts and practice words

SUGGESTED USE: Excellent for use as word wall categories headings and lists, whole class review, in literacy centers for practice, review on vocabulary, spelling, sentence and story writing prompts.
Can also be used for individual review as the 4" x 5" Individual Study Cards (See below.) Students may prefer the larger cards and print.

978-0-9771101-7-9   Pat Doran's *Phonics Steps to Reading Success A Fast-Paced, Word-Attack System for Developing and Improving Reading Skills* [PSRS], 4th Ed.
Individual Study Cards, 4th Edition

- Approximately 4" x 5" for individual use and learning centers.
- Full color, glossy card stock
- Includes consonant sounds' chart, phonics concepts and practice words.

SUGGESTED USE: For small group or individual, review and homework study and in literacy centers for practice, vocabulary development, spelling, sentence and story writing prompts.

Acknowledgements

With thanks to Chris Doran for his patience and generosity,
Lisa and Jeff Cragg, Yasmine, Jeffery, Kellan,
Peter B. and Dafina Doran,
Jean-Marie Doran,
Joy Doran

Special thanks to
Jacqueline Anderson and Janet Martin for their friendship and wise advice and
to Lisa Cragg and Joy Doran for their many hours of assistance, effort,
gracious enthusiasm, and encouragement.

☆ Special Note of Appreciation ☆ *Thank you to* JEANNIE ELLER *of Action Reading for her dedication, enthusiasm, and inspiration. Some ideas, organization, and linguistic design of Phonics Steps to Reading Success were inspired by George O. Cureton, Action Reading, the Participatory Approach, Allyn and Bacon, Inc., Boston, 1973, www.actionreading.com.*

Self-esteem begins with the ability to read efficiently and fluently.

Teach others how to read and their future will have no limits!

-Kent Looft
Design Arts

CONTENTS

LESSONS

Use this section of contents for Chapter Two as template to record information for date/class/lesson, etc. This Table of Contents may be duplicated.

Page

1. **Short vowel sounds**   _____/_____/_____
   To provide short vowel practice.

2. **Mixed-up short vowel practice**   _____/_____/_____
   To provide mixed short vowel practice.

3. **Short vowel stories**   _____/_____/_____
   To show how easy it is to read short vowels/long words
   and comprehension practice.

4. **-ck Sounds**   _____/_____/_____
   To teach the short vowels with -ck.

5. **Spelling -ck words**   _____/_____/_____
   To teach the spelling of sounds not letter names.
   To provide spelling practice using __ck words.

6. **-ck word practice**   _____/_____/_____
   To provide practice, increase speed and accuracy.
   To provide __ ck word reading evaluation.

7. **Bad Speller? Why?**   _____/_____/_____
   To provide encouragement and possible reasons
   Why individuals think they are bad spellers.

8. **Words with *le* at the end**   _____/_____/_____
   To demonstrate correct reading and
   Spelling of -le words.

X

90. *de-* = down, from, reverse action
   dis- = apart

   _____/_____/_____

91. *ex-* = out, out of, outside of
   in = in, put in

   _____/_____/_____

92. *in*, il, im, ir = not

   _____/_____/_____

93. *inter-* = between, among
   *intra- /*Intro- = within

   _____/_____/_____

94. *mis-* = wrong

   _____/_____/_____

95. *per-* = through

   _____/_____/_____

96. *pre-* = before
   post- = after

   _____/_____/_____

97. *pro-* =for, before

   _____/_____/_____

98. *re-* =again, back

   _____/_____/_____

99. *se-* = aside, apart
   sub- = under, below

   _____/_____/_____

100. *super-* = above
   trans- = across, through, beyond

   _____/_____/_____

101. *un-* = not
   uni-, bi-, tri- = 1,2,3

   _____/_____/_____

102. **More prefixes**
   Introduction to other prefixes

   _____/_____/_____

103. *i before e except after c*
   To teach this important spelling rule

   _____/_____/_____

104. **-ie Troublemakers**
   To teach the reversal of the Team Talkers
   with some *ie* words.

   _____/_____/_____

APPENDIX

PREFACE

The purpose of reading is the successful comprehension of an author's words. Yet, educators frequently hear from parents that, "My child can read, but he (or she) has trouble with comprehension." Why then do so many individuals struggle with accurate comprehension? With so much time and money spent on reading instruction, how is this possible?

To understand why a student might struggle with comprehension, it is helpful to imagine him sitting on a three-legged stool. If all of the legs are of equal length and strength, the student will sit comfortably with ease. However, if one of the legs is weak or not as long or as strong as the others, the student will labor to keep his balance, embarrassed at his wobbling. Should we consider the student to be "sitting disabled" or a "struggling sitter?" Clearly the answer is no. Therefore, when the student is taught ineffectively to use the essential three "legs of comprehension," should he be considered as reading disabled? Often, this is precisely the case.

When it comes to reading instruction, the three *legs* of reading comprehension are
accurate reading of the written words, understanding of the meanings of the words, and **sufficient background knowledge**, including facts, concepts, and conventions of grammar.

While Pat Doran's PHONICS STEPS TO READING SUCCESS is not a complete *reading* program, it is a fast-paced, *word-attack* skills program that quickly helps build two strong "legs" necessary for successful comprehension, namely, **accurate reading** and increased **vocabulary knowledge.**

WHY DO SO MANY PEOPLE HAVE TROUBLE WITH READING?

Over the past few generations, millions had been taught to read using unproven and experimental reading methods. Even today, many teachers unknowingly use these approaches. These techniques may teach students to guess at words, to use illustrations to "figure out" what a word might be, to skip words, or to memorize long lists of whole words by their shape. These latter are usually called "sight words" or high-frequency words.

Sometimes good strategies are looped together with less-than-good strategies. This is when theorists, working with publishing companies, combine ideas from various effective with non-effective approaches to come up with "new" approaches. However, there is now a universe of data from long-term, rigorous, scientific research showing what is most effective. This approach requires that phonics concepts are presented directly and systematically and that students learn to blend sounds with *accuracy* from left to right, from beginning to end of the words.

Often, in the effort to get students reading early, "sight-words" and non-explicit phonics instruction may be taught. It may *appear* to be effective in the early primary grades. However, such non-phonics instruction can lead to persistent errors that students make as they use these strategies beyond primary grades. When students later employ these *error-causing strategies* to tackle reading tasks in upper grades, students frequently become frustrated or resign themselves to failure. Still others are mislabeled as being in some way *disabled*. It may be that some of these students are skilled at using ineffective strategies or were never given the tools.

WHAT IS PHONICS AND WHY IS IT NECESSARY?

Reading English is like unlocking a code. Letters are symbols that stand for sounds. When we teach phonics, we are teaching the students to look at a symbol and say the sound that "goes with" the symbol. Therefore, the symbol <u>b</u> as in <u>b</u>at says /b/. There are 26 letters in the alphabet and approximately 44 sounds made by those letters or combinations. These represent the basic phonics code of the English language.

When students are taught to read using phonics, they can unlock the code as they read across each word. This is called **de**coding. When students are taught to say a sound in a word and write the letter or letters that "make that sound," this is **en**coding. It is how words are spelled.

Of course, the English language is not "pure" English. It is a rich, fluid language, boasting the influence of many others, such as Latin, Greek, German, French, Old English and Middle English. Thus, many words in modern English cause trouble and do not follow standard rules. While the pronunciations of consonant sounds have remained relatively stable, the variations, pronunciations, and spellings of vowels within some words have *shifted* or changed over time.

Therefore, most of our problems in reading and spelling English words are caused by vowels. *PHONICS STEPS TO READING SUCCESS* [PSRS] focuses primarily on the study of vowels. This phonics, word-attack program is designed for students who already know their consonant sounds.

If the student does not know the consonant sounds, these sounds must be learned *before* beginning the program. This book includes a consonant and vowel chart at the end of this section. The instructor can purchase a set of study cards, such as the PSRS Study Cards. In addition, it is possible to create consonant cards using a picture of a **b**at for b pronounced /b/, **h**at for h pronounced /h/, **r**abbit for r pronounced /r/, and so forth.

HOW DO STUDENTS LEARN THE WRONG STRATEGIES?

As mentioned above, non-systematic or non-explicit phonics methods suggest that students should memorize many words by their configuration, their shape, or "how they look." Often, these sight-words are combined into lists. Such lists contain *high-frequency* words that regularly appear in books and reading passages. Examples of these frequently-appearing words are *on, no, was, saw, in, it, if,* and *is*. This approach has been referred to as *anti-phonics*. It is the opposite of decoding. Nonetheless, it is a practice commonly used in today's classrooms.

Unfortunately, the similarities of word shapes can be confusing to readers of all ages. This is a common cause of reading and comprehension errors. What's more, the long lists, often containing hundreds of high-frequency words, can be very difficult to memorize. This leads to additional confusion, guessing, and comprehension errors when reading. Is "He saw the dog," the same as "He was the dog?" Rather than memorizing these words "by sight" students should be taught the meanings of these high-frequency words through aural/oral instruction until the students can learn to read (decode) most of these words which are highly decodable.

When students are taught to use explicit phonics, they do not memorize words. Instead, they decode letters' sounds from left to right. This eliminates the guessing game. Using this phonics-based approach, even so, students will encounter some words not easy to decode such as *was*. Unlike the lists of hundreds of memorized sight-words, these exceptions thankfully are limited and can be taught as "troublemakers" – words that tend to "break the rules." Once students are aware of the troublemaker word or word parts, they do not have to estimate at meanings or sounds. Accuracy takes the place of unwanted and error-causing strategies such as guessing.

In spite of everything research has revealed to us, many reading programs still promote sight-word memorization of regular or decodable words such as *saw*. The practice of *sight memorization* was originally an offshoot of methods used to teach deaf students under the direction of the Reverend Dr. Thomas Gallaudet. Since students with a hearing disability could not hear the letter-word sounds, Gallaudet provided a work-around solution that focused on rote memorization of visual word shapes representing pictures or concepts. When this method is modified and used to instruct students who do not possess a hearing disability, it is very problematic. It frequently leads to a situation whereby students with no actual disability become *instructionally* disabled.

Sometimes, students are instructed in a hybrid approach. In this way, they are introduced to *some* phonics concepts, but are also told to use rely on instant recognition of familiar words as whole units or as parts of words. The approach still requires students to *guess at words*, *substitute words*, or simply *skip words*. Under this method, students may be encouraged to pronounce the sounds of the first few letters in a word and then to *make up* the rest of the word *as long as it makes sense*.

This strategy is an example of what can be identified by the acronym **CAPs**, namely, **commonly-accepted practices *without any validating research to support their use*.** Unfortunately for many students, they carry the burden of having been taught to read using a variety of ineffective CAPs. In fact, often CAPs only serve to *cap* the reading and academic advancement of otherwise capable learners.

Developers and implementers of these strategies do not *intend* for students to make mistakes. However, in the push to have students read too early and quickly, they are encouraged to "read" books or passages long before they have acquired the phonics skills that are required accurately to read all of the words in a given text. In response, students tend to invent their own "survival" strategies. Reading therefore becomes a slow, burdensome balancing act filled with frustration and weighed down with guessing and errors.

Confusion enters. Comprehension is impeded.

If these "error-causing strategies" are not identified and corrected, the consequence of deficient and ineffective reading skills learned in school become a lifelong problem. Therefore, it is necessary to provide readers with fast, effective, efficient decoding strategies at the very beginning of their reading instruction. On the other hand, if the damage already has been done, explicit, systematic and direct instruction of effective strategies must be the focus of intervention. This is especially relevant for students who are labeled as "learning (reading) disabled" or "struggling readers." Interventions that focus on reinforcing ineffective strategies such as guessing and dependent reading only serve to cement the error-causing inefficiencies. Often, intervention approaches serve only to make accommodations to the reader's current abilities rather than provide effective instruction to correct what is lacking or ineffective.

On the other hand, when students are taught the phonics concepts systematically through explicit, direct instruction, most struggling students can acquire the skills to blend letter sounds, left to right, with an accuracy that will lead to the fluency. Ultimately, with practice, the accurate and automaticity of decoding skills will be in place. That "leg" of comprehension will be strong.

Does This Mean That Learning Disabilities Can Be Corrected?

If a student's disability is not caused, for example, by a physiological factor, but rather an educational one, the answer is yes. Note that in primary grades, the level of reading materials is strictly controlled. At first, a student's reading difficulty may not be obvious. Words are still basic. Pictures and illustrations provide a number of contextual clues. As noted above, this is one reason why non-phonics or anti-phonics strategies initially may *appear* to be effective.

However, as an individual advances through school and reading matter becomes more difficult, comprehension will suffer. A student's test scores will be far below his or her capabilities. In many cases, these students will assume that the problem is their own. Meanwhile, dedicated parents or teachers may assume that a student *dyslexic, learning disabled* or is simply prone to "mistakes" or "not trying hard enough." In fact, **the reader simply and *effectively* may be using the error-causing strategies that he or she has been taught to use**.

One solution to this problem is to provide students with the tools to unlock the language code using phonics. Pat Doran's *Phonics Steps to Reading Success* program is therefore a first step to better reading and comprehension that begins with accurately reading the written word.

When teaching older students, instructors must stress the importance of *unlearning* ineffective strategies by *learning* to read phonetically. Still, **a few foundational steps are necessary regardless of a student's age or ability.** This core skill set, taught systematically, will be the basis for continued success and will replace old, faulty strategies. Yet, old methods like guessing or substitution may be hard to unlearn. Patience on the part of teacher and student is essential.

Do I Need to Have a Phonics Background To Teach PSRS?

It is not necessary because this is foundational phonics information that has been taught and learned in various ways for generations by skilled and unskilled individuals alike. In fact, PSRS was designed for ease of use. On the lessons' pages, instructors with various skill levels -- from teachers with extensive backgrounds to parents who are trying to find ways to help their own children -- will find useful tips they can use throughout the program. Just read the information aloud or explain it clearly to the student(s). Remember to follow the detailed suggestions found on the pages just preceding Chapters One and Two. Other instructions appear on each page of the program. Page-by-Page Helpful Hints also can be found in the Appendix.

Using Phonics Concepts to Read with Accuracy and Fluency

It is essential for educators to understand that PSRS is a skill-building program and not a complete reading program. As with learning any new skill set, knowing how to decode the English language though phonics is not enough. Students must practice these skills, receive instructional feedback to correct errors, and be supported in efforts to apply their new knowledge.

Independent reading of decodable text is necessary for each learner to develop accuracy and fluency. The goal is for the student automatically to read through words they encounter. It is generally not an effective way to develop reading skills by listening to books on tape, having the teacher or an adult be the reader as the student "follows along" or does echo or "parrot reading." This is particularly true if the student is not able to decode the words independently.

It is true that student *may* benefit somewhat while "reading along" as the teacher models fluent reading. The student *may* gain a bit of advantage in repetition and recitation. Also, cooperation with other students in a small group or learning center projects *may* offer a bit of review options. However, the focus of instruction must be on teaching every student how to sound out new words and passages accurately, fluently, and independently. To that end, the student will be able to become a self-sufficient, life-long reader only when he or she has skills to read well, applying without help basic phonics concepts unconsciously and automarically.

Keys to a New Car – Learning a New Skill

Thus, reading instruction can be compared to giving a teenager the keys to a new car. Simply having access to a car or even being an observant passenger is not enough. New drivers will also need to know the rules of the road, have supervised practice, and know how to skillfully apply their knowledge in a safe environment. They should practice skills like breaking and merging into traffic multiple times. But practice not only "makes perfect," as the saying goes, it makes permanent. This is the role of the instructor: to ensure that correct procedures and habits that will be foundational for the future are instilled in a new driver from the beginning.

When I learned to drive, my teacher provided direct instruction. He required that I study a driving handbook to learn the rules. Next, he tested my mastery of the rules. One weekend, we went to an empty campus parking lot where I applied these rules under his guidance. I drove diagonally across the lot and applied the brakes only when told to do so. My instructor warned me to follow the rules exactly and with accuracy. In that way, I would avoid hitting any poles with his new car.

At the time, it felt like I was speeding, even if we only traveled at the brisk pace of 5 miles an hour. At a slow, safe speed, I learned to master these new rules and tools. I continued to practice these techniques and gained experiential knowledge of how a car reacts to my direction and the many dangers to anticipate. Before I even attempted street driving, however,

I had to answer a quiz on the rules of the road. When I ventured onto real roads, I drove slowly and with caution. My instructor sat in the passenger's seat and would correct any errors or oversights. This supportive practice challenged and strengthened my skills in a variety of situations.

In contrast to this guided supervision of my driving, the method by which I was taught to sew was quite different. Instead of careful instruction, I was shown an example and was left to work out the kinks on my own. I may have been a very good driver, but my sewing was a disaster. In the same way, teachers should *rely less on modeling* for students on how to read effectively and more on putting students in the "driver's seat" and having them apply what they have learned. Students must become **independent**, **accurate**, and **fluent** readers. They can learn to read with automaticity only by repeated, independent practice. Teachers must be in the supportive role as they teach, merging the "rules of the road" (phonics decoding) with the same kind of "hands-on" guidance that young drivers receive as they practice and develop mastery.

When applying this principle to reading instruction, there are effective and ineffective methods. For example, some educators have been taught to urge students to model the teachers' own advanced, fluent reading. In this way, a teacher will read a passage of text, after which their students will provide chorus of "parrot reading." Some students may indeed read along. But others will recite only what their ears have detected. Still others will pretend to read while hiding their own deficiencies. In a classroom, there is safety of numbers. But what will happen when reading deficiencies carry over into adulthood? Sadly, this is the experience of millions of adults. It is one that today's instructors energetically should aim to prevent. As will be demonstrated later, there are ways to use the most effective forms of these strategies, while avoiding less effective pitfalls.

Regardless of their reading ability, many students may internalize the wrong lesson when the teacher *models* or is the lead reader for most reading tasks in class. Instead of identifying aural (hearing) comprehension with the written word or the teacher's fluency, students may internalize a much more basic lesson: "Teacher reads fast." Consequently, students will often attempt to copy the instructor's speed but not their accuracy.

Much like my own experience in sewing, by mimicking the example of an expert, I overlooked basic, technical details. This might have produced some hilarious experiments in my fashions, but I have survived life without being able to create my own clothes. In practice, my survival strategy is to shop for clothes instead of sew them. It is a strategy that has served me well. In contrast, reading instruction is an entirely different and far more serious matter. Unlike sewing, literacy education should not be something that a student "picks up" by observation or guessing in a hit-or-miss fashion.

Reading instructors should therefore place readers in the *driver's seat*. Students must be given countless opportunities independently to hone their accurate reading and decoding skills. They must be able to apply the rules and tools of the phonics code. Much like driving, they should be prepared for highly irregular or new situations (words) and not be surprised or startled by "troublemakers" they might encounter on the road.

Once students learn the phonics code though PSRS, they will have the skills to decode almost any text. But reading is a skill that must be practiced. The teacher's role in PSRS is to teach, guide, and provide instructional feedback as students --no matter what their ages--make progress.

It seems quite improbable to many that PSRS is effective for learners ages 9-109. Nonetheless, while the systematic, synthetic blending PSRS system is effective for young and old alike, obviously, younger students and English-language learners will require a slower pace with more review, vocabulary development, and decoding practice than will older learners or English speakers. Post primary students can go much more quickly through the program, often in 10-20 hours. Review is essential for all. If possible, teach PSRS at the beginning of a school year or semester so that students will be more prepared to handle required reading tasks. The instructor may want to use the optional PSRS Study Cards as classroom word-wall categories, and/or for whole class or individual daily or weekly review, or as an extra tutoring strategy.

FROM PHONICS STEPS TO READING SUCCESS

To read and succeed, students must be able to decode words accurately. Of course, **vocabulary development** and **sufficient background knowledge** are essential, too. However, once students have completed the reading and spelling tasks of PSRS, they will be able to decode almost any word in the English language. Frustration and errors of the past will diminish and eventually disappear. Accuracy, automaticity, and fluency will rise as will comprehension and self-esteem.

Similar to the experience of first learning to drive, practice and repeated application of new skills and knowledge of rules will be required. Re-reading is a valuable strategy, one that is proven to be effective – and even necessary. It can be done using the following suggested techniques.

RE-READING STRATEGIES FOR ACCURACY AND FLUENCY

✐ STRATEGIES IN A CLASSROOM SETTING: For whole class, large and small groups

1. Teach the research-proven approach of systematic, synthetic decoding (reading) and encoding (spelling) strategies used in PSRS. Review the concepts daily by use of referring to concepts previously covered or the phonics concepts' study cards.

2. To avoid error-causing strategies, use only decodable materials for reading texts, namely, texts that require the students to use the phonics concepts learned thus far.

3. Foster a **positive classroom environment** by:
   a. Developing an atmosphere of respect in the classroom, explaining at the beginning of the year – and reminding throughout the year – that all students have different skills. Students will work individually and as a team to help support and guide students to achieve their highest potentials.
   b. Explaining to students that every member of the class has different needs and may need varied help and instruction because everyone learns in different ways and we *all* make mistakes. [You may want to share an experience of, for example, how YOU, as an adult, needed someone's help and had to call roadside assistance when you locked yourself out of the car with the keys inside or made a mistake when you burned a holiday meal.]
   c. Never permitting disrespect in the classroom.

    d. Developing mutual respect and have meaningful, simple class mottos such as:
       "AT EVERY MOMENT, DO WHAT RESPECT REQUIRES."

4. Lay the foundation for reading of decodable text by:

    a. Discussing or explaining **essential background knowledge** with which the students may not be familiar. [Note: Grammatical concepts also are part of that background knowledge that aid in comprehension. Include capital letters, clauses, punctuation, transitional words/ phrases, dialogue, etc.]

    b. Developing an understanding of the **vocabulary** used in the material.

    c. Discussing and analyzing troublemakers **and irregular words** that readers will encounter. You can include vocabulary words like "Chicago" or other *high frequency* troublemakers such as *was, I, to, the,* and *does* that may be taught as "sight words." [Note that you can help students understand that parts of these "sight words" or troublemaker words follow phonics rules and some parts of the words do not.] Suggested solutions for teaching "sight words":

       • Help students identify the parts of these words that are decodable.

       • Help students identify the "troublemaker" parts.

       • Practice highly-irregular high-frequency *sight* words in decodable contexts, not in long, meaningless lists:
         "He **was** hot." "**They** run." "**The** dog sits." "He **does** not run."

5. Involve **all** students in the reading aloud. [The teacher might consider randomly drawing names from a jar or employ *'round robin* reading. See re-reading strategies below.]

    a. **Exception:** If a student is new to the class and has not had phonics decoding instruction -- or you have not yet determined his/her decoding mastery -- explain that in the future, soon, the student will be reading with the class.

       1) Then, of course, it is up to you, the teacher, to be certain the child is taught the essential decoding skills quickly and as soon as possible.

       2) Use PSRS as your fast-paced approach for you or a trained volunteer to teach to any new student(s).

    b. **Groups:** If possible, use similar-ability grouping strategies, not mixed- ability grouping.

       1) Raise the bar of excellence for every student.

       2) Do not lower the reading assignments for stronger readers to accommodate the needs of weaker readers.

    c. **Do not lower expectations** for weaker readers simply by making *accommodations* that often only serve to impede reading advancement. [**Do not modify** or reduce, as a general practice, the amount of required work to be done by these students. Do not, for example, accommodate for lack of skills by assigning 5 spelling words instead of 10. Teach the skills. **Do not assume** that the student has been taught correctly in the past.]

    d. The teacher must do the following:

       1) Assess decoding knowledge, skill-level, and accuracy/fluency levels.

       2) **Determine** what students don't know and **teach** what is lacking.

       3) Work with parents and volunteers who are taught how to aid advancement.

6. Depending on circumstances, as students are chosen to read, each should read a single sentence or paragraph of a decodable story, reader or textbook. [Do not assume the publisher's idea of decodable is accurate. YOU must be the *gatekeeper* who makes that determination based on your students' decoding knowledge, mastery, and skills.]

    a. If the one sentence/paragraph is too brief, the student should read two sentences or paragraphs.

    b. If the student struggles with the material, the teacher (not another student) may read *softly* through the word or sentence with the student. Depending on the circumstances, the teacher may use the errors as a "teachable moment" noting that we all require a little extra help once in a while. The teacher may do the following:

1) Stop the reading to say, "This is a concept with which many of you in class struggle. Let's review this concept before we continue." [**Briefly**, re-teach and review. Then, thank the student for permitting you to interrupt his/her reading time for this class instruction and have student continue reading.]

2) Continue with the procedure of students' reading of the sentences or passages, but you should identify which strategies the particular student(s) will need to have reviewed or re-taught during small group, one-on-one time with teacher, at lunchtime, or after school.

7. The whole group rereads the single sentence/paragraph that the student has just read.

8. A new name is drawn to select the next student or you may have the next student in the row or group read a sentence or paragraph. The process continues.

9. Choral reading of the entire sentence/passage should follow once each student has finished but before proceeding to the next passage. **Be certain all students are reading aloud and not simply "hiding" in the group by** *pretending* **to read.**

10. Comprehension questions can be interspersed throughout the reading and, of course, at the end, everyone does choral reading of the *complete* passage.

11. The teacher must provide a *decodable* practice assignment, *decodable* quiz, or follow-up assessment to be certain that all students can comprehend what they have read.

   a. Assuming that the text is perhaps only 2-4 paragraphs, the students should be given a **decodable** handout that will test their reading comprehension.

   b. Every student's **individual** reading and comprehension skills must be assessed.

      1) Variations in strategies can be included in reading and assessment.

      2) Do not assess an individual student's comprehension and decoding abilities based on group activities without evaluating the individual's achievement as well.

   c. While students are working on the worksheets or assignments, the teacher may walk through the room, assisting any students who may be struggling, frustrated, unsure, or have questions.

   d. If a teacher finds that a student requires help, the teacher may want to indicate the area on the student's paper with a star or a motivational stamp, such as a *happy face*. This will identify for the teacher the specific place where assistance was needed. This technique has many benefits:

      1) For the teacher, the indicator serves as an embedded code, noting which skill set(s) a particular student may not have mastered.

      2) For the student, the location of the star or stamp will seem random, much like the stamps which all other students receive.

      3) The comprehension worksheet or assignment will also serve as a screener for teachers, identifying which students understood the material, their ability to respond to written questions, and where each student requires extra help.

Caution: When students practice re-reading and/or use rhyming, predictable books, it may appear that they are "reading" the material. In actual fact, students may be only reciting memorized passages. While there is value in recitation, we must not confuse it with reading. Be aware of this potential obstacle in popular reading-curriculum material. **For homework, do not give non-decodable assignments. Homework is to be decodable and to be practice of learned strategies.**

🖉 STRATEGIES IN A TUTORING SETTING

1. Teach PSRS decoding (reading) and encoding (spelling) strategies.
2. Consistently review the concepts that have been taught in previous lessons.
3. Primary students, ELL, and special ed students may need more processing time. In these cases:
   a. PSRS decoding/ encoding instruction or task-completion requires a slower pace.
   b. Students may need to practice with more decodable text in order to reinforce previous concepts, and lay the groundwork for ones that will be introduced later.
4. Post-primary students who are required to engage in higher-level reading tasks in other classes will require a faster-paced approach to learning or reviewing phonics concepts. PSRS decoding and encoding tasks may require a faster pace for instruction.
   a. Students may need to focus on vocabulary development.
   b. If time is limited, nonetheless, teach PSRS concepts from **beginning to end**.
   c. Do not select lessons randomly; teach systematically in the order they are in PSRS.
      1) You want to be certain no "holes" are left in the phonics knowledge.
      2) Review concepts before each session.
      3) Encourage the student(s) to use phonics concepts in any reading activities associated with other classes or outside of school.
      4) If time permits, once the students have completed PSRS, follow the re-reading strategies above.

🖉 STEPS FOR SILENT READING AND RE-READING STRATEGIES FOR BEGINNING READERS

1. Provide a **decodable** passage or story and review any vocabulary or necessary background knowledge before students begin silent reading.
   a. Permit students to mark words for phonics concepts, if possible. For example:
      Over short vowels that "say their sound" students may denote "ă."
      For long vowels that "say their names" they may mark the letter "ā."
   b. Students may cross out silent letters as in words with silent e at the end or vowel, as in case of "tēams." (See PSRS page 13.)
   c. Students may use arrows on the text. (See p. 22.)
   d. Students may put boxes around diagra ph s. (See p. 46.)
2. Students should then silently read their passages at least **three** times.
3. After silently reading, students should then read their passages aloud to the teacher.
4. As necessary, students may then read aloud the class, small group or a partner.

🖉 STRATEGIES FOR SILENT READING AND INDIVIDUAL READING BY POST-PRIMARY READERS

1. Students should have three books on their desks: a dictionary –personal, if possible-- a fiction book, and a non-fiction book.
2. When students are finished with assigned work, they should do individual, silent reading.
   a. When students encounter any unfamiliar words, they should use their dictionaries, highlight the word and meaning or, if they cannot write in the dictionary, they can write the word and meaning in a journal. [If they don't know the meanings of the words in the definitions, they can continue to look up those words. Your students can become word detectives or word scholars.]
   b. At the end of the day or week, you may want to give tests, have the students to share new words, use them in a sentence, and/or share some new information they learned.
3. A good motto for you and the class to follow is to **NEVER WASTE A LEARNING MINUTE.**

For you and your students, **"It doesn't matter where you come from; it matters where YOU decide to go!**

Vowel, Consonant and Other Sound/Symbols

Linguistics tell us that "**short vowels**" take less time to pronounce than do "**long vowels**." Thus, we have the terms, "long" and "short" vowels. Explain to students that the "short" and "long" diacritical marks over the vowels are used as pronunciation aides in the dictionary. Vowels are formed with an open mouth; consonants are pronounced by stopping and releasing air in various ways.

ă	ā	sh
ĕ	ē	ch
ĭ	ī	th
ŏ	ō	this th
ŭ	ū	ow
er ir ur	-oy oi-	aw au

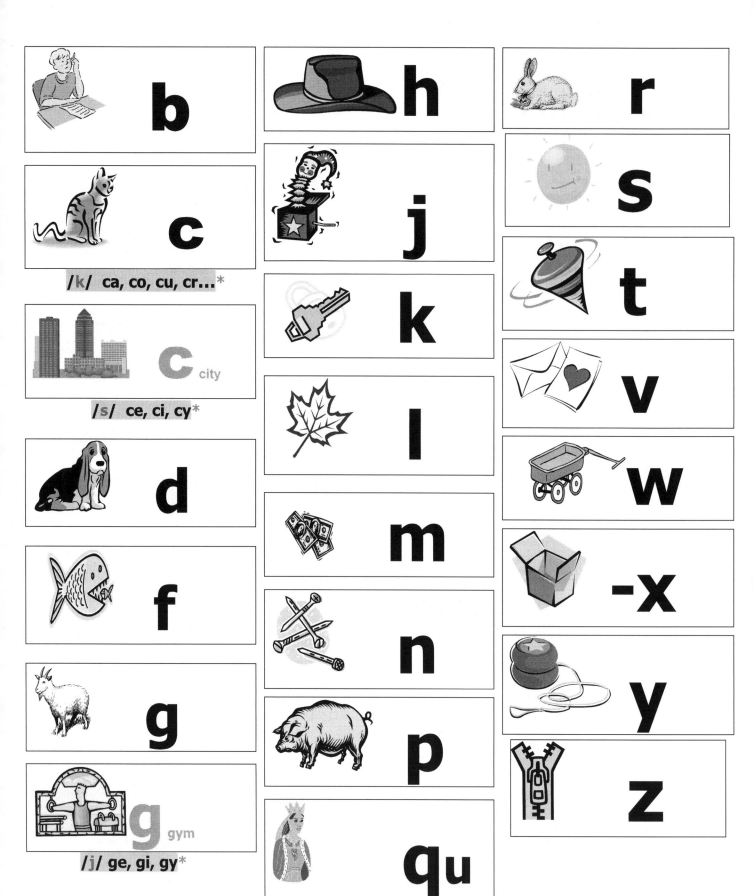

b

c

/k/ ca, co, cu, cr...*

c city

/s/ ce, ci, cy*

d

f

g

g gym

/j/ ge, gi, gy*

h

j

k

l

m

n

p

qu

r

s

t

v

w

-x

y

z

* Say ch in choo-*choo* and *church*. See PSRS, p. 43. Also see p. 60 -65.   ** Exceptions such as *target, girl, give*. See PSRS, p. 67.
*** The letter x at the beginning of a word may sound like /z/ as in *xylophone* or "x" as in *x-ray*. **Look in a dictionary for pronunciation help.**

PHONICS STEPS TO READING SUCCESS CHECKLIST

EASY PROCEDURE: WHAT DO I TEACH AND HOW DO I TEACH IT?

FOLLOW THESE HELPFUL HINTS THROUGHOUT THE PROGRAM. MORE SPECIFIC INSTRUCTIONS ARE ON EACH PAGE. SIMPLY READ THE INSTRUCTIONS ALOUD OR EXPLAIN THEM TO THE STUDENT(S). THIS IS A COMPACT, FAST-PACED PROGRAM FILLED WITH INFORMATION AND SKILLS' INSTRUCTION. IF YOU WOULD LIKE OTHER SUGGESTIONS FOR THE TEACHING OF CHAPTER ONE AND CHAPTER TWO, THEY CAN BE FOUND IN APPENDIX (PAGE-BY-PAGE HELPFUL HINTS, BEGINNING ON P. 107).

☐ **Read instructional material clearly, with expression and enthusiasm.** It is acceptable for you to ask very fluent, advanced readers read *some* of the instructional portions.

☐ **Ask the students if they understand and/or have any questions regarding instructional material.** It may be that instructions will be better understood as the word lists are read. As necessary, review concepts by returning to previously-taught lessons. You may want to use flashcards for a quick review of concepts.

☐ **Facilitate the fast-paced decoding of the words and lists.** Decoding is pronouncing the *sounds* of the letters as they appear in the word from beginning to end. **Use a pointer or your finger as a guide under or over *each* sound as it is pronounced, left → to → right.** Do not place pointer at the *middle* of the word. Always start at the first sound of the word, then glide, left to right, to the final sound.

☐ **Pronounce some of the words softly along with the students as the lists are read, but do not read the word first and then have students repeat after you.** There is value in recitation and "echo reading," but it is not the same as independent reading/ decoding.

☐ **Point out and discuss with students any words or parts of the words that may cause problems in spelling.** Encoding is writing the letter(s) English requires for each sound. Remind students that they need to be *active readers* and as they are reading, they should take note of spelling *troublemakers*. Learning to be a good speller may take more time and effort to master than will decoding.

Remind students that there may be a "code overlap" where similar sounds have different spelling such as **ay** in **pay**, **ae** in **maelstrom**, **ai** in **rain**, **eigh** in the number **eight**, and **a-e** in **pane**. In spite of this confusing aspect of the English language, students will become better spellers as they develop an understanding of the code used in English. People who know the code are better readers *and* spellers. As students read words, they will identify those words that have troublemakers. Do not have students memorize words by configuration. PSRS students have the tools to become good spellers!

☐ **Give a short spelling review/quiz after each page or column.** While the focus of PSRS is to teach phonics concepts needed for accurate reading, do not omit spelling quizzes.

Important Tips for Giving Spelling Practice "Quiz"

(1) Pre-select 3-8 spelling words.
(2) **Help students to pre-analyze, to identify tricks or troublemakers in these words.** (This teaches students how to study words to develop accurate spelling.)

(3) Give practice quiz.
(4) During the quiz, students may say sounds quietly, *sounding out* as they write letters from beginning to end.
(5) Correct and analyze errors. Affirm success/progress. (See procedure for correction below. You may always reinforce the concept later.)

☐ **Allow students to self-correct by comparing their words to the correct words from the list.** Permit students to make the corrections, either by crossing out the word and writing it correctly to the side or just correcting the error within the word.

☐ **Ask which students got 100 %. One wrong? Two wrong? Who is improving?** Congratulate success and progress. Students are "competing" with themselves, not each other.

☐ **Ask for volunteers to share the words they got wrong.** Thank student(s) for volunteering. Remind them that this helps everyone to analyze errors since everyone in class is a learner. If students are uncomfortable about sharing at first, you may ask students to "make up" an error they think someone might make.

☐ **Put the incorrect spelling on board/overhead.** Example: The correct word is *tape*. The student wrote *tap*. You or the student can pronounce the word as it is written. Ask, "What do we have to do to make a say its name?" or "What do I have to do to change *tap* to *tape*?" After analyzing a few mistakes, thank students for volunteering and continue. Move through the program quickly. You may always reinforce concepts later. (See pp.115 ff.) You may want to encourage or assign outside "homework" work for spelling/vocabulary development.

Chapter One

Introduction to

"Short" Vowels

"Short" Vowel Sounds

a

Ann's **a**pple

e

Ed's **e**gg

i

In the **i**gloo.

o

Ox says, "Ah."
Open wide.

u

Umbrella is up.

📖 As you read across, *left → to → right*, you must clearly pronounce EACH letter's sound.* Notice how the shape of your mouth changes as each letter's sound is pronounced, one right after the other, across the word, *left → to → right*. Use a finger or pointer under each sound as you read. Look back at the Short Vowel Sounds' graphics page if you need sound-picture clues to remind you of the sounds to make for the vowels.

map   zet

bin   sod

tud

*Hint for:
° Teacher: When you give spelling words, enunciate slowly. Exaggerate as necessary.
° Student: To spell, softly say each sound in the word aloud slowly as you write each letter or letters as you say the sound.

As you read across, *left → to → right*, you must clearly pronounce EACH letter's sound. Notice how the shape of your mouth changes as each letter's sound is pronounced, one right after the other, across the word, left → *to* → *right*. Look back at the "Short" Vowel Sounds' graphics page if you need sound/picture clues to remind you of the sounds to make for the vowels.

mapontazet

binrumsod

wanitudimsan

*See suggestions at the bottom of Page B.

As you read across, *left → to → right*, you must clearly pronounce EACH letter's sound.* Notice how the shape of your mouth changes as each letter's sound is pronounced, one right after the other, across the word, *left → to → right*. Spelling: Say the sounds as you write each letter (symbol).

dat   **zet**

tik   **pom**

fud

*See suggestions at the bottom of Page B.

📖 As you read across, *left → to → right*, you must clearly pronounce EACH letter's sound.* Notice how the shape of your mouth changes as each letter's sound is pronounced, one right after the other, across the word, *left → to → right*. Look back at the "Short" Vowel Sounds' graphics page if you need sound/picture clues to remind you of the sounds to make for the vowels. You simply read one sound at a time.

datponizet

tiksanpom

lamifudimsan

*See suggestions at the bottom of Page B.

(Pages F-G are optional. Use as needed.)

As you read across, *left → to → right*, you must clearly pronounce EACH letter's sound.* Notice how the shape of your mouth changes as each letter's sound is pronounced, one right after the other, across the word, *left → to → right*. Look back at the "Short" Vowel Sounds' graphics page if you need sound/picture clues to remind you of the sounds to make for the vowels. Each word here has three sounds.

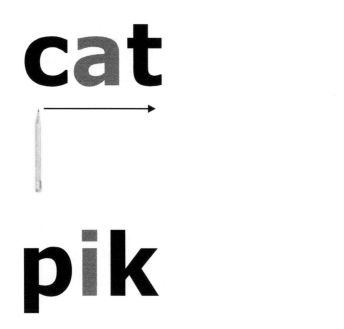

cat

pen

pik

dot

bun

*See suggestions at the bottom of Page B.

📖 As you read across, *left → to → right*, you must clearly pronounce EACH letter's sound.* Notice how the shape of your mouth changes as each letter's sound is pronounced, one right after the other, across the word, *left → to → right*. Look back at the "Short" Vowel Sounds graphic page if you need sound/picture clues to remind you of the sounds to make for the vowels. Remember that you don't have to read the word as a whole. Read the single sounds across the word, one at a time.

catpanupen

piksadadot

tunbunron

*See suggestions at the bottom of Page B.

Chapter Two
DEVELOPMENT OF VOWEL
and WORD ATTACK SKILLS.

The instructor should read aloud or explain the informational material on each page in an interesting manner. The instructor may want to use a pointer to allow the students to follow along *if* the informational material is being read to them and is large enough to read. There are over 5,500 words in the lists.

Important! Do not omit informational material for the student(s).

* Read word lists as a group or *'round robin* with each student taking a turn. Teacher should model reading words *left to right* and have the students repeat after him/her only for the first three words in a list.
  * It is not helpful for students to repeat entire word lists <u>after</u> a teacher reads each word.
  * When this is done, student(s) may just repeat what is *heard* instead of *reading* from *left to right*.

* Correct any pronunciation or articulation errors.

* All students must be actively following along and participating.

* **Keep the lessons moving quickly!** Return to review pages briefly or as needed for review once program is completed.

* Remember to have a three, five, or eight--word-spelling quiz after most lessons as marked followed by self-correction and analyzing of errors.
  * Students may <u>volunteer</u> the misspelling of a word so they and others can become skilled in identifying / correcting errors.

* Be positive and encouraging!

* Remind students to apply what they learn throughout the day, in other classes or activities such as shopping, cooking, etc.

As you are working with the students(s), you may preview and pre-analyze spelling words for quizzes. Spelling quizzes in PSRS are to be used to reinforce left-to-right phonics concepts to re-teach concepts when necessary. Note: See page 113 of the *Page-by-Page Helpful Hints* in the appendix. You may want to make a classroom poster of these hints for students to use frequently as a ready-reference.

When a vowel is the **only** vowel in a word, it says its *short* sound.	Think about the SHAPE of your mouth as you say vowels.	1. Read all sounds across. 2. Blend sounds from first to last.	Ox says "Aah," *NOT* "Oh, nO!" for these *short-O* words.	T After all lists have been read, skip around for drill.
# a	# e	# i	# o	# u
fast	bed	fit	hot	dust
map	bent	mist	pond	spun
tan	red	slip	cot	bump
flat	test	pin	Don	hunt
trap	desk	twist	rob	stun
bat	spent	hint	fond	pun
mat	felt	fist	got	must
Sam	jet	if	lots	trust
cap	lent	lip	on	trunk
clap	blend	sip	mom	junk
clasp	sped	strip	blond	grunt
damp	slept	bit	font	strum
drag	west	grip	prom	plum
ask	ten	in	spot	grump
dad	pen	split	pots	
hand	sent	trip	stop	
lamp	vet	tip	stomp	

T Spelling practice with 5-8 words. Enunciate slowly and clearly. **Analyze errors.**

Spelling: 📄✏

Mixed-up Short Vowel Practice

- When you read words, read across, left to right.
- Read each sound as it appears in the word. Emphasize the last sound clearly, also.
- Do not add sounds!   Do not leave out sounds!   Do not guess at a word!

an	fond	ask	trust
ten	blast	sip	ax
in	hat	run	bank
on	stand	fast	step
up	fun	sun	Ann
dent	fret	Ben	flop
fan	plum	cup	zip
slat	blimp	rod	lap
slot	pump	list	dog
pin	swim	rust	it
pan	if	rob	fib
stomp	bump	trap	Sam
pond	flat	stamp	
pun	Stan	past	
fin	stump	Pam	
Ted	buzz	bond	

⇨ Names begin with CAPITAL letters. Find names on this page.
T After EACH spelling quiz, analyze/correct errors. Spelling:

What? "*the* ™" is a TROUBLEMAKER! It says, "*Thuh*."

The ™ usually stands for "Trademark." However, in this program ™ will indicate a type of *troublemaker*. When troublemakers are introduced, they will also be highlighted in green.

Hint: If "the" comes in front of words that begin with a vowel, say "thee."

Try words beginning with vowels and pronounce the as *thee*: the apple, the egg, the ox.

SHORT VOWEL STORIES

T COMPREHENSION TECHNIQUE: It may be helpful to have students illustrate this silly story.

Ted sat on the bed. The fat dog sat on Ted. The red cat sat on the dog. The flat hat sat on the dog. The mat sat on the flat hat. Ted had a flat bed.

Is the hat fat or flat?	[ ] fat	[ ] flat
Is the dog fat?	[ ] yes	[ ] no
Is the mat on the hat?	[ ] yes	[ ] no

Answers: flat   yes   yes

Bob is a cat.   Bob is in the tub.
Ann is a tan dog.   Ann is not in the tub.
Ann is on the bed.   Bits is a mad cat.
Bits is on a mat on the bed.   Stan is a big man.
Stan cannot get in the tub.   Stan cannot get on the bed. Ann is on the bed.   Bits is on the bed.
Bob is in the tub.   Stan just has to stand.

Is the cat in the tub?	[ ] yes	[ ] no
Is Bob the man?	[ ] yes	[ ] no
Is Stan on the bed?	[ ] yes	[ ] no

Answers: yes   no   no

Was this work hard? Of course not! Can you read this next word?

Annisonthebed

📖 You can see that it says **Ann is on the bed.** Sounds of letters are pronounced across words, left to right. To read, **blend** the letters' sounds. They flow like water from one sound into another.

The clock says "Tick, tock."

-ck ™ **Spell with two letters: ck.**
Read as *one sound*: **/ k /.**
Can you read *short vowel* **+ ck sounds?**

ack, eck, ick, ock, uck

Most words with short vowel and /k/ sound at the end will have the –ck teammates at the end.

▶ **We'll learn later that the ck follows rules, but can be trouble when it comes to spelling words with -ck correctly.**

T **When you spell words with SHORT VOWEL + ck, write sounds that you hear as you hear them.**

📖 **Now, let's practice reading aloud. Underline short vowel + ck if necessary. Change the shape of your mouth as you read each SOUND.**

t<u>ack</u>	neck	tock	brick
s<u>ack</u>	peck	stock	wick
tr<u>ack</u>	fleck	smock	Nick
Mack	speck	block	tick
black	deck	mock	pluck
pack	flock	stick	stuck
plack	clock	Mick	duck
flack	pock	Rick	muck
rack	lock	pick	tuck
slack	rock	trick	truck

Spelling after p.5.

SOUND SPELLING SENSE

1. **Take your time.**
2. **Write slowly.**
   3. **Write sounds as you hear them.**

📖 **Here is a silly word: *smick***

1. Say the *SOUNDS* left to right. */s/ /m/ / i / / k /*

2. Say the *SOUND* as you write….*sssss.* Write the **letter s.**

3. Say the *SOUND* as you write… *mmm.* Write the **letter m.**

4. Then, say to yourself, "*I hear a short i (igloo) sound and / k /
   sound. I must remember to write i c k.*" Write: *s m ick.*

📖 Remember the **short vowel sounds** + **/ k /** are usually written

   ack   eck   ick   ock   uck.

T Practice spelling with silly words. This activity will give students practice in spelling words with which they are not familiar. Students can learn to use phonics concepts. This will prevent guessing or inventive spelling. There is no need to memorize whole words. Use the following silly words to model spelling with the ck™. Students can say each sound aloud softly as they write, remembering *-ck* .

Practice spelling: **plock   blick   smuck   spock**

Ask how the *name* of Doctor Spock would be written? (Names begin with capital letters.)

T For the following spelling test, do not let students see the words until spelling words have been written. Then, let students see each section and correct their own work.

👉 To pronounce and read the WORDS clearly and carefully you must pronounce each SOUND clearly and carefully.

Spelling: 📝 1. **sick**   2. **stick**   3. **brick**   4. **smock**   5. **block**

T Students may correct their own work, but if there are errors, discuss reasons for misspelling. You want students to practice and to succeed!

Congratulate successes. Analyze errors.   Be positive, but be sure to **stress accuracy!**

After reading each group of words below, you may give a short spelling test for each set.
Uncover one set at a time to give students an opportunity to self-correct.

Can you read and spell the words on this page?

ack eck ick ock uck

Read quickly and accurately.

Try to increase your time and number of words correct on each section.

1. **sack, sick, sock, suck**
2. **back, bick, bock, buck**
3. **rack, Rick, rock, ruck**
4. **tack, tick, tock, tuck**

16 possible   Reading time:_____   # right _____   # wrong_____

1. **Mick, Mack, muck, mock**
2. **lock, luck, lick, lack**
3. **pack, peck, pock, puck**
4. **zuck, zock, zick, Zack**

16 possible   Reading time:_____   # right _____   # wrong_____

1. **seck, tick, rock, pack**
2. **muck, back, rock, tock**
3. **zuck, Nick, tock, buck**
4. **lick, tack, bick, pock**

16 possible   Reading time:_____   # right _____   # wrong_____

1. **stick, stack, stock, stuck**
2. **stock, brack, rock, stuck**
3. **brick, brack, brock, bruck**
4. **trick, truck, lick, pock**

16 possible   Reading time:_____   # right _____   # wrong_____

Pick up the big black sticks. Stack the sticks on the rocks. Sit on the black sticks.

16 possible   Reading time:_____   # right _____   # wrong_____

Can you increase <u>accuracy</u> and <u>improve your speed</u> a second or third time?
Success is achieved by improving a little bit each time you do something!

What?

📖 Yes, some students are taught to spell by memorizing the patterns and shapes of letters in a word.

Spelling practice activities may have students try to match those words to fit into boxes. Letters may be <u>in</u> a word, but in the wrong place!

When is a girl a gril?

The answer is: Never!

📖 **DO YOU THINK YOU ARE A BAD SPELLER?** You may have learned this way.

Is **g** i r **l** the same as **g** r i **l** ?

If you read and spell sounds from **left to right**, you will not make this kind of error.

T **See below how the words** *was* **and** *saw* **fit into the same boxes.**

The letters are all lower case. There is a letter *a* in the middle. The letters *s* and *w* are on either end. If students do not read or write from *left to right*, it is easy for them to remember that there are the letters *a, s and w* in the word. However, they might not be able to remember the order in which the letters are written.

This may explain why some people write words using the correct letters, but put letters in the wrong places as with **girl / gril** or **saw / was.**

Top Secret! You can read and spell correctly. ALWAYS start at the beginning.
Spell and read from left → to → right !
This extremely important skill must be reinforced constantly!

Is **w** **a** **s** the same as **s** **a** **w** ?

HERE IS A SPELLING TROUBLEMAKER!

It is easy to handle a bundle
of words with *le* at the end.

If an *le* is at the end of a word,
you must say the / l / sound as in *bundle*.
The e is silent. It makes no sound.

E at the end of any word with another vowel is ALWAYS silent.

★ Words with short vowel sounds *usually* have
two consonants before the *le,* as in the words
bundle or ***meddle***. This rule is **not** for words ending in ***able / ible***.

WHAT? **Sometimes people think that the *le* sounds like an ō.**
Say *can-dle*, not *cand-o*.
Always pronounce carefully.

Speak clearly and you will spell better!

T Instruct students to read the following words. **Preview/pre-analyze the words that will be in the spelling quiz. Have student identify double letters, *silent e*, etc.** This will help students understand how to improve spelling awareness. Give spelling quiz. Students check their own work when they are finished. **Congratulate success. Analyze errors.**

bundle	handle	saddle	crackle
settle	meddle	peddle	paddle
sprinkle	twinkle	single	tingle

Only a few words ending with /l/ are spelled with –*el*. Examples: nickel, bushel

T Students may read the following sentence or you may try it as a sentence dictation:

He held a bundle of candles in his little hand.

CAN YOU READ LONG NONSENSE WORDS?

📖 Sometimes students are told to guess at a word.
GUESSING CAUSES MISTAKES!! With phonics, this is not necessary!

• This exercise is to help you read each sound from *left ➜ to ➜ right*.
It will also help you to use the CONTEXT to find meanings of words.
CONTEXT means the parts of a sentence or paragraph *that occur before and after a word or words*. Sometimes context will not be of help.
Sometimes we must use the dictionary.

Students should read across from *left to right*. As they read aloud, they should form their mouths to make the sound of each letter in the order that it appears in the word. Remember, *le* says / l /. If another vowel is in the word, the *end e* is ALWAYS silent.

s p a n f a n b i s u t t l e

Use context clues below to learn the meaning of this silly, long word.

Tom drives his red pick-up s p a n f a n b i s u t t l e. It has no locks. It is not a safe s p a n f a n b i s u t t l e to drive. He frets.

What is it? (Truck?) What clues did you use? What do you think "fret" means? (Worry.)
Is it a real word? Could you use a dictionary or just context to determine its meaning?

s i p s w o n d u n d l e

Can you find the meaning for this made-up word by using context clues?

My little brown s i p s w o n d u n d l e had five puppies.

No one would have thought it was an apple, a table, or a pencil.

i n e x p r e s s i b l e

Context helps. For real words, you might have to use a dictionary if clues are not clear.

When Sam was told that he was about to meet the world's greatest football player, his joy was inexpressible. Sam could not describe his feeling to anyone. His excitement was beyond words. Was he happy or sad? What clues did you use to decide?

Read the following story. Option: Teacher may <u>tell</u> the story to explain concept.
When using a color version, review this helpful pronunciation color code:

BLUE = *SHORT SOUNDS*   DARK RED = *VOWEL NAME*   OUTLINED / GRAY = Silent *VOWEL*

THE TEAM TALKER VOWEL STORY

In the Land of Letters, vowels played by saying their sounds. At first, vowels were so bashful that they would play alone, only saying their sounds. They did not play together. They were too shy.

One day A ran into E and they began to play next to each other. E was brave.

E made up a game with A. At first, A was its usual shy self in the game. A only wanted to say its sound /a /, as in *apple*.

The vowel **E** was bolder and had even more courage when it was with **A**.

E said, "I'll give you ALL of my courage. Then, you can say your name. I'll stand by you. Have my courage!"

E said, "I'll be like a silent shadow. Look for me. When you see me behind you, say your name. I'll be silent, but I will be so proud of you. You will talk for BOTH of us. We will make a great team.

You will be the TEAM TALKER, and I'll be your silent partner."

They tried it, and it worked! With **E**'s courage, **A** could say its name.

E now acts like a shadow friend.

You can see it, but it is silent.

THIS WAS A FUN NEW GAME!

E stayed next to its teammate.

A had **E**'s courage to say its own name.

E was silent! **A** was the FIRST VOWEL of the team.

Therefore, **A** was the "TEAM TALKER."

E became the silent, shadow vowel.

Soon, the other bashful vowels joined in.

They called this their *Shadow Game*. At first, many of them were too shy.

They would only say their sounds, /e/, /i/, /o/,/u/. Playing the Shadow Game was fun!

Vowels teamed up with each other. The first teammate now had courage! It was the TEAM TALKER. The second teammate was silent. It could be seen but not heard.

Vowels often changed teammates. In these new *vowel teams,* the first vowel said its own name ā, ē, ī, ō or ū. Its teammate, the silent shadow vowel, could be seen but not heard.

Other letters in the land saw this game and would say an old saying:

"WHEN TWO VOWELS GO WALKING,
THE **FIRST** ONE DOES THE TALKING."

TOP SECRET!

**Occasionally, troublemakers do not follow the rules. We will hear about them later.
Until then, just follow the rules of the SHADOW GAME.**
LET THE VOWELS BE THE BOSS. THEY ARE IN CHARGE.
IT IS *THEIR* GAME!

📖 **Say the name of the <u>first</u> vowel only.
The team talker says its letter name, ā, ē, ī, ō, or ū.
The shadow vowel says nothing.
The shadow vowel is seen but not heard.**

āe̶   ēe̶   īe   ōe   ūe

āy   āi   ōa   ēa   ūi

📖 **The FIRST VOWEL gets all of its courage from the second vowel. The first vowel says its own NAME.
When you read, read across the word from *left to right*.**

T **IMPORTANT!! Put a line over the first vowel to mark the team talker.
Cross out the silent vowel.** This strategy is very helpful!
Students may use the lines for help as needed. Read each sound across the word as demonstrated below with the arrows.

A dictionary will show a "long vowel" that says its name with a line over it.

Read:

Team Talkers with Silent Shadow Vowels

📖 **Students say the name of the first vowel only. The second letter's sound is silent.** Teachers may read with the students for <u>first few words only</u>. Students must practice reading **independently**.

ā e   ē e   ī e   ō e   ū e

ā y   ā i   ō a   ē a   ū i

The Team Talker is ē in the ēa Team.

1. s <u>ēa</u> m
   | seam |

2. l <u>ēa</u> n
   | lean |

3. l <u>ēa</u> f
   | leaf |

4. s <u>ēa</u> l
   | seal |

5. h <u>ēa</u> l
   | heal |

Practice with this team.

If necessary, mark the vowels as above.

b<u>ēa</u>m

t<u>ēa</u>m

dr<u>ēa</u>m

cr<u>ēa</u>m

steam

lean

seat
Jean
speak
feast
beast
treat
bead ✎

T Some *ea* words break vowel team rules. Many come from other languages and have changed. You may have to read **short e with** silent a as in **br<u>ea</u>d, thr<u>ea</u>d, w<u>ea</u>ther, h<u>ea</u>d, l<u>ea</u>d.**

Try both ways or use a dictionary.

T The following words have a *ture* slur when the *tu* is said. Slurred sounds make it difficult to spell correctly. Here are some hints to help:

1. **Pronounce clearly.**
2. **Exaggerate pronunciation:** fea – **ture**
3. **Pay attention to troublemakers. It is easier to spell.**

T Note that crea**ture** comes from the Latin word, creatura. There is no slur in Latin. Each sound was said clearly. ☐ Model the English spelling. Say the sounds as you write f-ea-t-u-r-e. Always write the silent shadow vowels.

The Team Talker is ā in the āy Team.

T Remind students to use color coding and diacritical marks. Do not use echo reading.

1. st **āy**

   stay

2. p **āy**

   pay

3. tr **āy**

   tray

4. gr **āy**

   gray

5. M **āy**

   May

6. pl **āy**

   play

7. s **āy**

   say

Practice with the āy team

Read across from left to right.

Read each sound.

Do not skip any letters.

Let the letters be in charge.

No guessing!

---

br**āy**

str**āy**

gr**āy**

---

away

splay

way

r**ē**lay

clay

Clayton

play

day

defray

delay

dismay

display

m**ī**slay

---

sway

lay

slay

essay

Ay alone says ā , never long ī.

However, "aye" sometimes is

pronounced ī.

" The pirate said, 'Aye-aye, Captain.' "

T You may want to practice new words and add a spelling review of a few words from previous lessons.

Review, preview and pre-analyze as necessary.

The Team Talker is ō in the ōa Team.

T Remind students to use color coding and diacritical marks. Do not use echo reading.

1. fl ōa t — float
2. rōast — roast
3. g ōa t — goat
4. s ōa p — soap
5. f ōa m — foam
6. b ōa t — boat
7. c ōa t — coat

Practice with the ōa Team

T If necessary, demonstrate the silence of the shadow vowel by drawing a line through the 2nd team vowel.

Also, draw the long diacritical mark over the vowel that says its own name.

Pronounce each sound. In the words below, the green dots are reminders that these are the letters that are "hit" or pronounced. Read across the word.

gōat
• •

sōap
• • •

mōat
• • •

T Use your own dots, lines, or arrows to remind students to read each sound.

Reading each sound across is an important skill to instill.

Do this throughout the program when necessary. It takes time and practice to replace any bad habits with good ones.

r ōa st
f ōa m
ōats
moan
groan
toad
coat
toast
float
load
goad
roam

T Ask students if there are any words that they do not understand. Simply tell them the meaning or model looking up some words in the dictionary. **Keep the lessons moving quickly.**

① Review **oa** concept. Preview and pre-analyze a few spelling words.

② Enunciate clearly to dictate words sound by sound.

③ Permit student(s) to enunciate sounds softly and *clearly* while writing letters. See p. 5.

④ Remind student(s) that spelling [encoding] is going from sound to symbol. It takes more awareness and study than reading [decoding] which is going from symbol to sound.

⑤ Remember **vowel teams** and **troublemakers**.

⑥ Analyze errors.

1. f āi nt
   faint

2. p āi nt
   paint

3. f āi l
   fail

4. t āi lor
   tailor

5. s āi l
   sail

6. m āi l
   mail

7. spr āi n
   sprain

Practice with the āi Team

📖 Read only the sounds that are not silent shadow teammates.

tail
mail
bail
taint
raid
hail
rain
drain
stain
rail
vain
sail

---

wail
wait
snail
gait
waist

brain
pail
strain
explain
hail

paint
fail
Braille
trail
nail
contain
maintain

📖 Now, read these five pairs of words.

The top word has a short vowel. The bottom word has a vowel team.

Add the silent shadow vowel i and read both words.

Brad
braid

pal
pa__l

pad
pa__d

mad
ma__d

rad
ra__d

The Team Talker is ī in the īe̱ Team

1. p īe̱ — pie
2. t īe̱ — tie
3. sp īe̱ d — spied
4. d īe̱ d — died
5. cr īe̱ d — cried
6. tr īe̱ d — tried
7. l īe̱ — lie

Practice with the īe̱ Team

died
fried
tried
tied
spied
cried

lied
pie
retried
plied
replied
dried
belīe̱*

* Usually **ie**™ at END of words says "ee," (*Marie*) and "*ies*," at end says "ees" as in *bunnies*.

The ēe̱ Team

1. m ēe̱ t — meet
2. f ēe̱ t — feet
3. sl ēe̱ p — sleep
4. d ēe̱ p — deep
5. str ēe̱ t — street
6. sl ēe̱ t — sleet

Practice with the ēe̱ Team

feet
flee
meet
seek
reek
sleek
meek
tree
free
see
seem
teem
creek
Greek
asleep*

Ⓣ * For ease of correct reading or spelling and to clarify any confusion, you may explain briefly -- but do not focus on -- "schwa e" as "usleep." Teach the basic phonics rules for now. Use dictionary as needed. 📝

Team Talker say ū in ūe, ūi, and ew™ Teams.

In some countries people often will pronounce strong long "u" for a *ui* team. In the U.S., we often read *ue*, *ui*, *ew*, with a bit more *ooo* pronunciation.

Try reading these words both ways. You may hear a British accent when you do?

1. d ū e

   | due |

2. st ew

   | stew |

3. h ew

   | hew |

4. s ūi t

   | suit |

5. S ū e

   | Sue |

Practice with the ūe Team

blue
true
clue
cue
glue
rescue
value
Sue
Tuesday
continue

📖 Sometimes two vowels are in a word together but are in separate syllables. They are sounded quickly but separately.
1. du·el 2. cru·el
3. fu·el 4. gru·el

Practice with the ūi Team

suit
fruit
suitor
recruit
suitable
recruiter

Practice with the ew says /ū/ Team

new
few
flew
Andrew
drew
crew
hew
news
renew
Lewis
askew
blew

📖 When in doubt, use rules you have been taught. Use a dictionary as needed.

Whichever way you pronounce *ue*, *ui*, *ew*, either as *oo* or long *u*, you will be correct. 📄✏️

The Team Talker is ō in the ōe Team.

T Remind students to use color coding and diacritical marks. Do not use echo reading. Use a pointer under each sound as it is pronounced.

1. d ōe
   [doe]
2. t ōe
   [toe]
3. al ōe
   [aloe]
4. D ōe
   [John Doe]
5. s ōe
   [soe]
6. P ōe
   [Edgar Allan Poe]
7. f ōe
   [foe]

Practice with the ōe Team

woeful
Joe
foe
ōboe
toenail
floe
roe
goes

does™ / duz /

📖 Some vowels are in a word together but are in separate syllables and are sounded separately.

dū-et
pō-et

T Names may be like tiny history lessons and may give clues as to how words were pronounced in the past.

The Greek *chi* = X, x, pronounced / k /. Some words and names have changed just a little or not at all over time.

The <u>ch</u> in the following name is pronounced / k /. It has two syllables, Chlo · e. Sometimes the e is pronounced. It is of Greek origin, and means "blooming."

You may find words or names that have old pronunciations that are used today.

T Use the following list for spelling practice.

Students may put a "long mark" over the first vowel that says its name and a line through the silent shadow vowel.

The second letter is silent when it is read. It is written for correct spelling.

Extra Vowel Team Practice

seam
coat
pail
foam
clean
suit
stew
meet

tried
trait
tree
toe
fruit
meat
Tuesday
feed

Remind students to use color coding and diacritical marks. Do not use echo reading.

Use a pointer under each sound as it is pronounced.

The ae team is not used often, but is necessary to know. These appear to be hard words but big words are easy. Read across. Look for vowel teams.

1. D āe mon

Daemon

2. G āe lic

Gaelic

3. Āe son

Aeson

4. j āe ger

jaeger

5. l āe ō tro pic

laeotropic

6. m āe l strom

maelstrom

7. t āe l

tael

Practice with all of the vowel teams.

dream
gray
toad
goat
contain
sundae
tied
replied
see
fleet
rescue
Tuesday
duel
recruit
suit
steward

Drew
flew
woeful
soe
aloe
Gaelic
essay
maelstrom
value
hew
spied
tied
lie
teen
queen
pail
mail
foam
goal

Sometimes a consonant can be found between a vowel and its silent shadow teammate e at the end of a word. A consonant may try to block the *courage* of the silent shadow teammate e and keep e's courage from getting to its vowel teammate. The consonant gets between the two vowel teammates.

A consonant wants to keep the first vowel shy and make it able to say its short sound only. It wants to split the vowel team.

The strength of silent SHADOW teammate e can get past ONE consonant blocker. With ONE consonant blocker, the first vowel team player will still say its name.

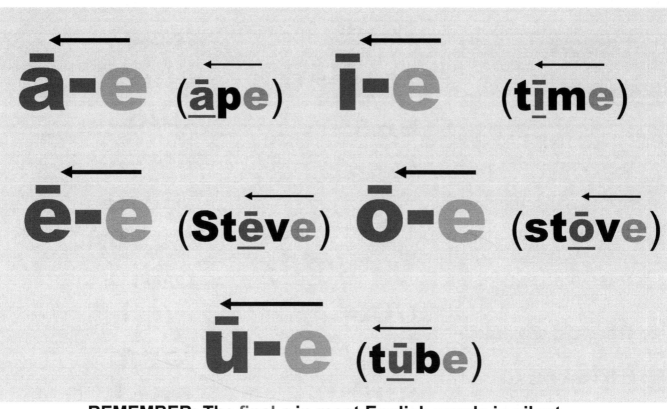

REMEMBER: The final e in most English words is silent.
The only time it is spoken is when it is the single vowel in the entire word.

he   me   be   she   we

TEAM TALKER with Consonant Blocker Practice:
Sometimes a consonant will try to get between the
silent shadow teammate e and its vowel teammate.
The blocker consonant cannot block e's courage.
The first vowel will still say its name.

Top secret! ALWAYS watch for the e at the end! The vowel partner will say its name. Read across the word. The last **e** is the strong, SILENT team member.

VERY IMPORTANT! <u>E</u> is the ONLY VOWEL that can send its courage past a consonant blocker to a teammate.

cān**e**	tube	slime
mān**e**	ride	hope
pān**e**	rote	stripe
plan**e**	kite	tape
Pet**e**	pale	line
snip**e**	bite	same
tim**e**	note	flame
hid**e**	fume	ripe

This is the
SHORT and LONG of It!
Careful practice makes perfect!

1. **can** **cāne**
2. **fin** **fīne**
3. **man** **mane**
4. **pan** **pane**
5. **plan** **plane**
6. **pet** **Pete**
7. **snip** **snipe**
8. **Tim** **time**
9. **hid** **hide**
10. **rid** **ride**

11. **rot** **rote**
12. **kit** **kite**
13. **pal** **pale**
14. **bit** **bite**
15. **not** **note**
16. **tot** **tote**
17. **slim** **slime**
18. **hop** **hope**
19. **strip** **stripe**
20. **tap** **tape**

Drill instills! Careful practice makes perfect!

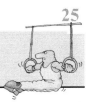

fast	grump	goal	not
bed	bet	beast	note
pond	stripe	steam	same
mist	main	jail	kite
dust	flake	pad	pane
fret	flack	paid	rid
ape	lump	deep	ride
track	Ben	sleep	dream
blue	truck	recruit	speak
boat	block	flue	relay
hope	stale	hew	float
Ed	candle	floe	week
pin	span	tael	waist
pen	brick	ax	Jane
glue	pluck	tax	few
spent	twinkle	ask	street
trust	defray	Kate	goes

Let's have some fun. Try reading silly *l o n g* words.

These nonsense words are decodable for you. You have all of the phonics facts you need to read them. You don't have to guess. **Word-guessing gets in the way of accurate comprehension. Change the form of your mouth to pronounce each sound (phoneme) in the order that it appears in each word.** Then, use the context to figure out the meanings. **For real words**, if context doesn't help, **use a dictionary**.

praitzanmayzepple

Today at breakfast, I had coffee, eggs, and a big plate of five praitzanmayzepples with fruit on top.

What context clues tell you what it is? Breakfast, plate, five of... (Could it be pancake?)

You didn't say *e*'s name, did you? The e in "zep" has no power. Also, remember that a shadow e at the end cannot send its courage past <u>two</u> blockers.

A few exceptions such as *hast*e, *wast*e, *past*e, *tast*e come from MIDDLE ENGLISH. In these words, the <u>a</u> says its own name.

vecklaipinkormaeple

Last year we had my granddad's 100th **vecklaipinkormaeple. People came and we had fun and ate cake. He had 100 red candles on his vecklaipinkormaeple cake.**

Was it his birthday? Did you use these clues? ...fun......cake...candles

WOW! **If you can read this 19-letter word, you can read ANYTHING! You cannot guess at these words. You don't have to.**

When you read and spell, let the letters be in charge.

1. **STUDY THE SOUNDS** in a word that might cause you trouble.

2. **PAY CAREFUL ATTENTION** to them. Make a mental note.

3. When you spell, **WRITE THE SOUNDS** in the order that you hear them.

4. **REMEMBER THE TROUBLEMAKERS**, what they are and where they are.

I SEE THE PLANE FLY IN THE SKY.

Tricky and sly words ending in y.

If a word has a y at the end, and
if there is another vowel in the word,
then, the y at the end says "eeeee."

SPELLING TIP: If you hear an "eee" sound at the end of a word, and
if there is ANOTHER VOWEL in that word, write the "eee" sound with the letter *y.*

Do not write e at the end!   SORE does NOT say SORRY.

📖 **When an e is at the end of <u>most</u> English words, it is silent.**
However, when words have only ONE SYLLABLE with ONE VOWEL that is an
e, the e is alone so it <u>MUST</u> SAY ITS NAME as in *be, me, he, she, we.*

happy	tricky	sadly	fifty	sixty
funny	bāby	™<u>qu</u>ickly*	sunny	fuzzy

The *y* acts just like a silent *shadow* e at the end. It will allow the vowel to say
its name. However, there MUST be 2 blocker consonants between the vowel
and the final *y* to keep the vowel from saying its own name.

→ SPELLING TIP: Two blocker consonants keep the vowel's *short* sound.
If there is just *one* consonant, DOUBLE it to keep the *short* vowel sound.

SPELLING TIP: Kitty is not kīty.   Bunny is not būny.

Practice! Take a spelling test. How well can you do?

📖 **If someone wants to write a word that ends in the sound
...eeee... as in *baby*, they should <u>say</u> /b/ /ā/ /b/ /eeee/
and then, <u>write</u> y at the end (baby).**
The word *baby* is <u>never</u> <u>written</u> babe. In *babe,* the end e is silent .

*Teach the ™<u>qu</u> as a troublemaker that says /kw/. More focus will be given to it later.

Y by ITSELF!

If it is by itself and is at the end, it is very proud and says, "I."

| my | dry | cry | fly | sly |
| sky | by | ™shy | fry | sty |

If it is at the end in a word with another vowel, it says, "*eeee*."

T Help students to identify which of the words have another vowel that will make the final y say "eee." Help students to pay attention to <u>double blockers</u> that will make the vowels say their short sounds.

1. The funny, fuzzy tricky bunny is shy as it sits by my bāby.

2. The man was happy, but shy as he won a dandy new car.

3. I am happy if I can get a ride in the sky and fly by myself.

4. The sly, tricky puppy rapidly ran to my flat boat to see it float by.

QUICK TEACHING MEMO:

Just as the y at the end of a word has a **long sound**, so does the O at the end of a word. When you see the *o* at the end of a word, say its **name** as in the following words:

go   no   so   CAUTION! Troublemaker Alert: ™ to

tomato   potato   solo   hello

Ⓣ For younger students, teacher should read and guide them through this skill as a **BRIEF** INTRODUCTION only. If students should encounter this troublesome y in the middle of a word, students will have some familiarity with it. **For these words with y**, the teacher may read all words softly **with** students, guiding as necessary.

What? **Sometimes *y* is a vowel between consonants.**
It could then sound like *short i* (igloo/ in) as in this old name:

Hippolytus

pygmy

gypsy

gymnasium

tyranny

_____

symbol

 Spelling trick to help you remember:
A **stop** sign is a **symbol.** Both words have **S** and **O**.

What? **Because of the y being used over time and by many people, sometimes *y* is a vowel between consonants.**

Then, it could sound like long i (kīte) as in this old name:

Siemon
Stylites

eye	tyrant	typhoon
type	typist	cypress

Note: You may hear other local dialects that pronounce the y as i (igloo) or ī (time).

These ™ psy words come from a Greek word which means *having to do with the mind.* The p makes NO SOUND.

When a word begins with psych, the *ch* = /k/. Thus, *psych* is pronounced as /sīk/.

™ psych · ol · ō · gy

™ psych · i · a · try

™ psych · ic   ™ psych

Vocabulary hint:

. -*ology* means the
   study of something.
. p s y c h e - refers to *the mind.*

What is psychology?

Answer: The study of the mind.

Bonus:
What is criminology? Symbology?

WORDS THAT ARE TROUBLEMAKERS!

Sometimes people say that English is hard to learn because there are so many words that break the rules. Let's find out! This page might help you to understand why.

Have you ever noticed that some people who speak English "sound *funny*" to you? You and I might pronounce <u>come</u> as /kŭm/. Some people from areas in England, Ireland or Scotland may pronounce it as /kōme/.

Some English-speaking people may sound differently to us or have "accents" because when they speak English, they may pronounce vowels differently than we do. Although they speak differently, we can still understand what they are saying.

Some words are very old troublemakers! They *turn away from* or *break the rules* that we are learning. They have changed. That is because some of these words have been in use for over 1,000 years. If you lasted over 1,000 years, you might change a little, too!

Wow! Some English words do break the rules. However, if you follow the rules when you read, what might happen is that you could have traces of British, Scottish or Australian accents. You would still be speaking correct English.

T   Have students read the eight troublemakers on this page using the rules that have been taught. For example: Read healthy with the <u>name</u> of e and <u>silent a</u> and <u>then</u>, with a short sound of e and silent a. Do students hear an accent? Often, different pronunciations of vowels result in local or regional dialects.

→   **Review troublemaker /th/.** Note that more attention will be paid to it later. You or the student(s) should read sentences.

1. ™ **healthy**	She is <u>healthy</u> and not sick.
2. ™ **ready**	I am <u>ready</u> to go.
3. ™ **come**	My dog will <u>come</u> to me.
4. ™ **instead**	I want an apple <u>instead</u> of candy.
5. ™ **heavy**	This big rock is <u>heavy</u>.
6. ™ **bread**	™Do you have milk and <u>bread</u>?
7. ™ **move**	Will you <u>move</u> the vase to the shelf?
8. ™ **weather**	Our <u>weather</u> is very hot.

PRACTICE WITH SOME TROUBLEMAKERS

Just as in any game, sport, or life in general, we need to learn to be around those individuals who do not like to follow the rules. Learn to outsmart them to avoid trouble.

Some words do not follow rules. Learn how to correctly spell words that cause trouble. You do not have to be bothered by them.

CORRECT SPELLING IS NECESSARY! YOU CAN DO IT.
You MUST study how the words are spelled!

1. **Say words the way they would sound according to the rules.**
2. **WHEN YOU SPELL, write each sound as you hear it.**
   - **When you read, pay attention to how words are spelled.**
   - **Notice where TROUBLEMAKERS are in the words.**

Be *word-smart* when you read. Combine reading/spelling awareness.

PRACTICE WITH THESE WORDS!

| healthy | ready | come | instead |
| heavy | bread | move | weather |

Reminder: *to* is a troublemaker. It says *"too."* You can teach words such as *to, you, one* and *does* as *troublemakers*, generally with some letters following the rule.

1. **Can you be _____ to go in one day?**

2. **Use a coat if the _____ is cold.**

3. **Jack is sick with the flu. He is not _____.**

4. **Can you _____ to my home?**

5. **The little pile of rocks is not _____.**

6. **He had to _____ to Texas from Maine.**

7. **We like to play basketball _____ of baseball.**

8. **I will get milk and _____ at the store.**

Answers: 1. ready   2. weather   3. healthy   4. come   5. heavy   6. move   7. instead   8. bread

READ THIS. IT MAY HELP YOU TO UNDERSTAND WHY ENGLISH SEEMS SO VERY CONFUSING!

Ⓣ **Scholars are people who study about many things. Scholars who study the English language know about many -- but not all -- of the origins or *beginnings* of English words. Some dictionaries give the origins of words. For example, the listed words below were taken from *Wordfinder*.***

This page is to introduce you to the reasons why some words "break the rules." Yes, there <u>are</u> reasons!

The English Language has a rich history, but that can cause problems for us. **The English we speak comes from a combination of Old English, Middle English, Latin, German and other languages. Many of the vowel teams like *oa, ea, au*, come from various languages.** That is why they sometimes break the rules that we know. This can be confusing.
→ This page shows some original spellings -- mostly Old English (OE) -- with today's spellings.

1. **active**
   actif

2. **they**
   thei

3. **your**
   eower

4. **promise**
   promys

5. **buy**
   buyen

6. **parents**
   parens

7. **shove**
   scufan

8. **above**
   a + bufen

9. **weather**
   weder

10. **wear**
    werian

11. **what**
    hwaet

12. **the**
    se, seo, thaet, thy

13. **head**
    heafod

14. **would**
    (OE) wolde
    (Archaic) **wouldst**

15. **feather**
    fether
- **As found in READER'S DIGEST OXFORD COMPLETE WORDFINDER,** 1996 Oxford Univ. Press.

 **Wow!** You don't need to carry a stack of dictionaries around with you to become a good speller! I have a better idea!

Be careful! A little inventive spelling causes <u>BIG</u> problems.

Most businesses will ask people to fill out a job application. Often poor spellers are not hired for many important jobs. Work hard so that you will become a good speller. People will respect your ability. You will be more confident when you write.

No excuses! You can do it. Pay attention to this helpful page.

EXAMPLE: **We may want to write:** *I like to eat bread and butter.* **However, be careful! The word, "bread," is a** *troublemaker***. The** *ea* **in this word breaks the rules. The first vowel DOES NOT say its name. It says its sound e (***egg***.) The second letter is <u>a</u> and is silent.**

→ **SPELLING TIPS: There are two ways to handle this troublemaker.**

1. Say the word in your mind by following <u>ALL</u> of the rules that you know.

This may *sound* strange to you, but this will help you spell correctly. In your mind, you will say "*brēₐd*."

This will help you spell the word correctly because you will remember that the ē will need a teammate.
→**Remember to put in the silent team member, *a* after <u>e</u>.**

2. The second way to spell correctly is to say the word as it is pronounced, but you must remember any troublemakers.

The dots below show you which sounds are written as they are heard. The arrow points to a silent spelling troublemaker.

You must make a "mental note" to remember where a troublemaker is.

b r e ₐ d
● ● ● ⬆ ●

T̄ **The *ea* team frequently is a troublemaker because many *ea* words come from other languages. You will only have to remember <u>one</u> troublemaker when you spell this word. What is it? (a)**

Hi! I'm Tricks! I'm here to help!

If spelling words are still giving you trouble, help is on the way!

Find **troublemakers** in words – **who** they are and **where** they are.
TRICKS can help you to remember how to spell a word!

Example: friend. *I have a friend in the end.* Spell: *fri - end*.

1. Learn that words like *sweat,* meaning *perspiration*, break the rules.

2. It looks like sw ē a t. It really says s w ĕ a t.

3. When you spell it, you may say the SOUNDS that you HEAR, but remember to put in that silent a after e.

Write SOUNDS from *left ⇒ to ⇒ right*.

You **only** have to remember the <u>troublemaker letters</u>.

Spelling is easy. "It's no sweat!"

Look for surprises like TROUBLEMAKER TRICKS in words!
Did you know that there is a **lie** in bel**ie**ve?
Did you know that there is an **ear** in your h**ear**t?

◆ Pronounce words in your head the way they are spelled.
Follow rules.
Notice tricks.
We pronounce this fa - vor - it. Think and spell fa-vor-īte.

Read from left to right ⇒ ⇒ ⇒ ⇒ ⇒

Read sounds from left to right.
Read words from left to right.

T The activity below reminds students to read from *left to right* and not to skip.

You are playing the letters' game.
Follow their rules. It's their game!

pail, paid, man, Sam, the, for

pail the for man paid the Sam

Sam paid the man for the pail.

📖 When you read lists of words, you do not skip around or leave out words. It is the same for sentences in dark gray areas. **It is the same for anything that you read. Practice this!**

sky, kite, can, I, the, see, the, in

sky in the kite the see I can

I can see the kite in the sky.

ALWAYS → read → from → *left* → to → *right*.
DON'T SKIP! DON'T GUESS. LET THE WORDS AND LETTERS BE IN CHARGE. IT IS THEIR GAME. READ BY THEIR RULES!

His picnic was rained out.
We say, "AW! That is sad! "

When you say the sound, make your mouth
shape like an oval egg.
Say, "Aw, aw, aw!"

THE ™AWESOME TEAM

Read these ™*aw* words. Notice that ™*aw* is in green.
Read across. Say each black letter's sound. Read ™*aw*.

Remember that it is EXTREMELY IMPORTANT to make your
mouth in an OVAL or egg shape when you say the aw sound.

dawn	paw	brawn
awl	craw	lawn
awe	flaw	tawny
raw	gawky	straw
law	hawk	pawn
fawn	bawl	drawn
awful	sprawl	saw

Spelling: 📄✏️

™Au is another ™aw sound!
™Au requires an oval mouth shape.

Arthur is an author.
Read each sound *left to right.*
Arthur is a name.
An author is a writer.

Read these au/aw words.

auto	autumn	applaud	Paul
author	haul	Maud	Audrey
Aubrey	automobile	Au' gust*	au gust'*

* Accent marks show STRESS or force. The accent mark (') in a dictionary tells us which syllables to stress. Words that are spelled alike can be pronounced a bit differently with a different syllable stressed.

rec ol lect´: **to remember**   re´ col lect: **to collect again**

com´ press: **a soft pad to apply cold or hot**   com press´: **to press together, condense**

Look in a dictionary for more.

TROUBLEMAKER ALERT! THE LETTER *a* AT THE END OF WORDS
WILL SAY THE / ŭ / SOUND.

Sometimes *i* comes before *a* or *u* in a word, as in *ia* or *iu*.

These are NOT the same as the shadow vowel teams a͟i or u͟i.

In the i͟a or i͟u team, i͟ will sound like the long ē (tree) sound and

a͟ or u͟ will say the short u (up) sound.

i a	Lidia	Austria	i u	mēdium	auditorium
↑ ↑	Australia	media	↑ ↑	pentium	folium
say			say		
ē ŭ	Maria	via	ē ŭ	radium	millenium

Top Secret! People in the United States might say **Aus-trā-lia.**
People in other places might say **Au-stral-ia.**   Spelling: 📄✏️

Stop! Don't run away!

You CAN read these!

When you say <u>au</u> or <u>aw</u>, make your mouth the oval shape. Try it. Remember that if you don't know the meaning of a word, use a dictionary.

1. **I s<u>aw</u> a dog with a sore p<u>aw</u> cr<u>aw</u>l onto the l<u>aw</u>n.**

2. **The l<u>aw</u>yer tried to dr<u>aw</u> the sun at d<u>aw</u>n.**

3. **Pick up the black sh<u>aw</u>l for my mother.**

4. **The ball hit him in the j<u>aw</u>. It was <u>aw</u>ful.**

5. **We saw his j<u>aw</u> get hit. He fell on the l<u>aw</u>n.**

6. **Sam had to haul the author's boxes in his automobile in the autumn.**

7. **Maud and Audrey can visit him in August.**

8. **Aunt Jan had to applaud Paul. He is an author.**
   You may pronounce "aunt" like "ant" or aunt. Both ways would be correct.

9. **Aunt Maud went to Austria and Australia.**

"SHORT" $\breve{oo}$:	"LONG" $\overline{oo}$:
foot	**moon**
book	**soon**
took	**moon**
nook	**boom**
hood	**fool**
look	**boot**
stood	**food**
wood	**goose**
good	**foolproof***
soot	**stool**
brookside*	**goof**
cook	**baboon**
	spooky
	hoop
	bamboo

Words with the same _oo_ sound:
should, would, could.

T These words are from Middle English and Anglo-Saxon spellings like **_scheolde, wolde._** Sometimes poets used spelling like **_couldst_**.

T This page is an example of the influence of dialects and local accents. There is a tiny difference in the <u>oo</u> sounds. The sound depends on how and where the words developed.

*COMPOUND WORDS are two words together to make one word: baseball, inside.

CONTROL YOUR CAR! *Look for r-controlled vowels.*

> Sometimes the letter *r* will change the sound of a vowel. It is a part of the shift of sounds through the centuries. It is called an r-controlled vowel.
>
> R-controlled vowels are ^{TM} troublemakers. They can be tricky!

a+r = _ar_ as in c_ar_	To read the word, *arm,* say: **/ah/ + /r/ + /m/ = a_r_m.**

If you are sounding out a word to spell, and you <u>hear</u> "r" as in <u>arm</u> or <u>c_ar_</u>, do not write *r*! **Write ar.**

T **HELPING CLUE:** If students are not sure, show them that they can underline the *ar* sound. **The <u>LETTER</u> "r" says "rr." The <u>SOUND</u> "r"= is spelled *ar*.** Reminder for the teacher: Do not read the words first and have the students repeat. Students should be doing independent reading (decoding).

arm	**sp_ar_k**
b_ar_	**tarp**
f_ar_m	**hard**
p_ar_k	**lard**
y_ar_d	**far**
st_ar_t	**tar**
Barb	**cart**
barb	**card**
dart	**yarn**
b_ar_k	**lark**
h_ar_m	

<u>A</u>re you sm_ar_t about <u>ar</u>?

It would be SMART to have a spelling practice test with these "r-controlled" vowels.

→ What is the difference between Barb and barb? 📝✏️

o + r = or  fork

This is easy! The *OR* TEAM always, always, always says *OR*!

f**or**	**n**o**r**mal
t**or**n	organ
b**or**n	forlorn
f**or**t	Horton
h**or**n	Morris
p**or**t	forget
st**or**m	conform
l**or**d	actor
fork	doctor
morn	afford
store	harbor
north	forever
stork	format
sort	inform
sport	

Preview and pre-study the words, noting any troublemakers. Study hint: <u>Horton</u> may be pronounced *Hortun*, but spelled Horton. 📝✏️

These r-controlled teams with NO SILENT SHADOW E will ALWAYS say *er, ir, ur*.

er Bert can serve.	**ir** Stir the tea.	**ur** I see rabbit fur.

er — Bert can serve.

mann**er**

herd

fern

verb

serpent

servant

perform

never

alert

after

perk

ever

offer

term 📄✏️

ir — Stir the tea.

g**ir**l	stir
f**ir**m	firm
bird	twirl
skirt	swirl
girls	dirty
skirts	sir
stirrup	fir
smirk	first
affirm	dirt
flirt	irk 📄✏️

ur — I see rabbit fur.

fur	burr
hurt	burn
burp	turn
spur	turf
hurdle	

nursery

absurd

purple

murmur

current 📄✏️

T Note: **ere**, **ire** and **ure** follow **VOWEL TEAM rules** as in here, fire, pure. 📄✏️

THE H comboS

More than 2,000 years ago, armies and tribes migrated into many areas. Most people did not have a written language. Many groups had picture symbols to represent the sounds in their words. Over years, people started using letters -- like the Roman alphabet that we use today -- for symbols to stand for the sounds in their languages.

Sometimes these languages had SOUND COMBINATIONS for which the people did not have letters. Over the years, the English language grew, using the Roman alphabet. For many reasons, TWO LETTERS were used as symbols to represent ONE SOUND. No one planned it this way. Because of usage, place of origin, sometimes confusion, sometimes poor writing, we now have two letters written for a particular sound. These are called digraphs:

di = two / graph = write.

c+h = ch as in choo-choo  /chips

The letter *h* was used to make many digraphs as with ch, sh, th, wh, ph.

T Each column uses less visual help. Make sure the student says a STRONG *ch* as in *choo-choo*, NOT soft *shoo-shoo*.

choo-choo
chain
chap
chip
chop
charm
chart
chomp
chill

cherry
chunk
cheese
cheek
Charles
chest
checker
churn
Chester

cheep
cheap
chin
chuckle
chump
chimp
chimpanzee
chimney

Top Secret!

☒ Do NOT say or spell *chim· i · nēy*.

☑ Correct = *chim · ney*.

Remember that when *c* and *h* are together, the same strong sound is usually heard that you hear in
choo-choo, chips, check.

Top Secret!

When a __ch__ sound follows a short vowel, you MUST have a blocker!

For example, in the word ra|n|ch, the n acts as a blocker.   If there is no blocker, you MUST put a t -blocker between the short vowel and the ch. In the word *ma|t|ch*, we had to add the t as a blocker. It slides into the ch sound as /tch/.

EXAMPLE: **Do not write** *mach*. **If there is no blocker, put in a** *t* **-blocker.**
Write: *match*.

Top Secret!

When a __ch__ sound follows a vowel team, you do not need to add blockers.

d|itch

p|each
VOWEL TEAM
No blocker needed.

r|anch

tr|ench

str|etch

m|atch

p|inch

l|atch

c|atch

sw|itch

gl|itch

Sc|otch

f|etch

sk|etch

Important!

A pitch·er
pitches the ball.

A pitch·er
of water.

A pic·ture hangs
on the wall.

Mark the words with the *short vowel + tch*.

Look for:
1. Long vowel teams
2. *-tch words*
3. Other blockers!

chin

stitch

luncheon

wretch

poach

catch

reach

flinch

hatch

ranch

trench

ditch

stretch

match

sketch

merchant

latch

watchful

teacher

hutch

bleach

archery

peach

satchel

dispatch

batch

hunch

etch

pinch

bench

fetch

arch

winch

T REVIEW RULES.
1. Long vowel teams
   —no blocker.
2. Short vowels must
   have a blocker.
3. If there is no blocker, put
   a *t* before you write *ch*!
4. Blocker rules apply
   to **-*dge* words** .

ridge   *sludge*

fidget   *grudge*

midget   *gadget*

edge   *ledge*

budget

📖 ALWAYS FIND OUT WHY
YOU MADE ERRORS – if
you have made any.

LEARN FROM YOUR
MISTAKES. Then, you
won't make them again.

This man will
*sh-sh–sh-sh*iver
**when he
*sh-sh-sh-sh*ovels snow!**

Why does *sh* NOT say the sounds /s/ /h/?

In 1066, William the Conqueror defeated the English king, Harold II, at the Battle of Hastings, and changed the language as well as the government of England. Probably, about that time, the *sc* was pronounced as /*ski*/ . The *sk* was changed to *sh* over time. Now we have the *sh* digraph.

THE STORY OF ENGLISH by Mario Pei, 1952, p. 84.

Could the changes have happened because of their careless handwriting? They certainly could not blame it on the computer spell-check program!

As you learn, you might want to put a box around or underline this tricky team.

ship	shōw	dash	shop
sheet	shelter	rash	fresh
sheep	shed	cash	shuck
shōre	shampoo	fish	sash
shall	shudder	gash	shape
shun	Shelley	lash	usher
shirt	shrub	mesh	shovel
shave	should	brush	
shade	sheen	trash	*TRY THESE!*
shame	hush	swish	dashboard
shrimp		shush	marshmallow
			seashore
			mushroom
			vanishing

CAN YOU READ THIS WRITING?

♦♒♓♦ ♓♦ ■□♦ ♒□□♎ ♦□ ♎□?

Many years ago, people used symbols instead of letters. The symbol for the *th* -sound was a picture of a thorn used by a group of people which we now call the *ancient Germanic tribes*. Today, we do not use picture symbols. We use letter symbols.

When the Roman *a/b/c/d* alphabet took the place of pictures, the *th* sound was written by two letters (symbols) because the Romans did not have the *th* sound in their speech or writing.

Now we have the digraph *t* + *h* = *th*. It started thousands of years ago.

The *th* sound can be *said* by softly sticking your tongue BEHIND your teeth and blowing as in

THANK you.

Sometime the *th* sound is "harder." Put your tongue BETWEEN your top and bottom teeth and blow, vibrating your tongue SLIGHTLY. This sound is in some words like *this, that, those, these, the.*

These 27 words have soft th.

1. thick
2. thank
3. thorn
4. thistle
5. thumb
6. threat
7. thread
8. thaw
9. three
10. thirty

Ask student(s): "Where do you hear the /th/ sound? In the beginning, middle or end?" Then box or circle the sound as shown in the first column.

11. thiēf™
12. bath
13. wrēath
14. mouth
15. thrifty
16. Smith
17. bōth
18. athlēte
19. author
20. Arthur
21. Rūth
22. cloth
23. death
24. north
25. forth
26. broth
27. path

Do not get caught in the ph /f/ typhoon.

The *ph* probably started thousands of years ago with the Romans in their Latin language and the Greeks in their language. WE CAN BLAME THEM FOR OUR TROUBLES!

Students can be reminded not to be afraid of big words. Read big words one sound at a time, from left to right, from beginning to end. This is a good page to use to look up some new words in a dictionary.

Remember: ph = /f/

1. **ph**one
2. **ph**antom
3. **ph**armacy
4. **ph**ase
5. **ph**rase

6. **ph**en·om·en·al
7. Ral**ph**
8. **Ph**yllis
9. ne**ph**ew
10. **ph**ī·al

11. **ph**legm
12. **ph**os**ph**orus
13. **ph**oto
14. **ph**otographer
15. **ph**otography

16. **Ph**illip
17. **ph**ysics
18. **ph**il·an·thro·py
19. dol**ph**in
20. sap·**ph**ire

21. ā**ph**id
22. **ph**il·har·mon·ic
23. ty**ph**oon
24. **ph**arynx
25. am**ph**ibian

26. **ph**ōtōstat
27. **ph**onics
28. **Ph**oēnix
29. gō**ph**er
30. Jose**ph**

31. so**ph**ōmōre
32. na**ph**tha
33. di**ph**theria
34. or**ph**an

35. **ph**lox
36. **Ph**ew!

The *wh* can be a problem!
When you read,
notice _w_ words.
Do they begin with the /w/
(as in *wagon*) sound or the /
_wh_ / (breath) sound?
Unsure of the spelling or meaning?
Consult a dictionary.

These words all have the *wh* breath *w*
sound. Put your finger in front of your
mouth. Blow slightly as you say *"whuh"*.
Feel a puff of air.
HAVING TROUBLE? Reverse the sounds
to <u>hw</u> to get the puff. IT MAY BE THAT
SOME OF THESE WORDS were once
spelled with a h w, <u>not</u> w h.
Did bad spellers cause us this
TROUBLE?

1. **whale**
2. **wharf**
3. **what**
4. **wheat**
5. **whatever**

6. **wheel**
7. **wheeze**
8. **wheedle**
9. **whelm**
10. **whelp**

11. **when**
12. **where**
13. **whether**
14. **whetstone**
15. **whew**
16. **whey** /*whā*/
17. **which**
18. **whichever**
19. **whiff**
20. **whiffle**

21. **Whig Party**
22. **while**
23. **whim**
24. **whimper**
25. **whimsy**

26. **whine**
27. **whiny**
28. **whinny**
29. **whippersnapper**
30. **whipping boy**

31. **whir**
32. **whirl**
33. **whirlpool**
34. **whirlwind**
35. **whisker**
36. **whet** [Not the same as wet.]

📖 THIS IS A GOOD PAGE TO USE A DICTIONARY.

TAKE TIME TO LEARN THESE ™TEAMS!
They are teams that try to confuse you!

The vowel looks like a *short* ĭ vowel,
but it is pronounced as a *long* ī vowel.
📖 Over 1500 years ago, the g and gh sounds were pronounced. Not now!

īld

Say i as in time.

wild
mild
child 📄✏️

īnd

Say i as in time.

find
remind
grind
kind
blind
binder
wind
behind
bind 📄✏️

īgn

Say i as in time.
The g is silent.

sign
design*
resign* 📄✏️

īgh

Say the i as in ice.
The g and h are silent.
Years ago they had been pronounced.

sigh
high
flight
might
lighten
bright

* You may hear people say dē-sign or design and rē-sign or resign.

brighten
tight
tighten
right
night
slight
mighty
sprightly 📄✏️

The following are
SHORT i teams.
They break the
īld īnd īgn igh
rules, but they follow
the igloo (in) / ĭ /
rules.

Context clues help with pronunciation.

1. We have to wind up some old clocks. ⏰

2. The soft wind is a breeze. 🌬️

TIME FOR REVIEW

Try these silly multi-syllable words.

📖 Sometimes you will see words that you have never heard before. Below are some silly words that will give you practice in reading long words that you have never heard before.

REMEMBER: **Read from *left to right* saying each sound.**
- **Say the vowel name in dark red.**
- **The silent shadow vowel says nothing.**
- **Say the short vowel sounds in blue.**
- **Remember vowel teams.**

1. **prēad·bēal·chēat**
2. **kwick·snick·chāy**
3. **chaisteatnew**
4. **kwaythaypain**

📖 IMPORTANT ADVICE!
READING UNFAMILIAR OR DIFFICULT WORDS?

1. **On paper or in your mind, follow the rules and mark the long vowels.**
2. **Cross out silent vowels.**
3. **Identify troublemakers, etc.**
4. **Change the shape of your mouth as you read each sound across the word, left to right.**

Now, words with no visual aids. Follow the rules. Read across.
Don't skip any sounds!

5. **stucktaystain**
6. **remindhighbail**
7. **fleascreamraid**
8. **spealpaymain**
9. **batbaitmanmain**
10. **mainbaitbatman**
11. **chainnewbeen**
12. **kwackpeckpen**

➔ Now, try spelling # 5 & # 6. First notice any troublemakers that you must remember. 📄✏️

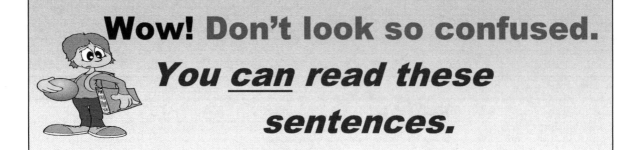

Wow! Don't look so confused.
You can read these sentences.

1. The w<u>il</u>d child was not m<u>il</u>d.

2. I f<u>ind</u> that I must rem<u>ind</u> the ch<u>ild</u> to w<u>ind</u> the clock.

3. A kind bl<u>ind</u> man went beh<u>ind</u> my window bl<u>ind</u>s to find his b<u>ind</u>er.

4. The city will des<u>i</u>gn Main Street's s<u>i</u>gn.

5. I find del<u>i</u>ght when I take a fl<u>i</u>ght in a br<u>i</u>ght airplane.

6. The s<u>i</u>ght of a bright l<u>i</u>ght may fr<u>i</u>ghten the child on the r<u>i</u>ght side.

Did you read these words the r<u>i</u>ght way?

ūe   ūi AND ew say ū

Stubborn-as-a-mūle review. These can be tricky.

That's right. Remember that
ūe ūi ew all say the letter name of ū.

In the U.S., we pronounce ui / ue / ew /ū/
with a bit more of a *moon /oo /* sound.
Try reading these words both ways. Do you hear a British accent?

ūe
1. blue   2. cue   3. clue
4. due   5. true   6. glue
7. Tuesday   8. Sue   9. sue   10. rescue

 ™ Remember how these words are pronounced?

cruel   fuel   duel   gruel

ūi
1. suit   2. suitable   3. fruit
4. suitor   5. re·cruit   6. suited

ew = **ū** Say the consonant sounds + U (oo).
Did you know that the letter w comes from old uu? Say double u!

few	grew	pew	chew	Drew
crew	flew	stew	drew	steward
news	threw	blew	renew	brew

You must study the spelling of these words so that YOU know
which ue / ui / ew to use. Remember that a diphthong is a
complex sound.
**Diphthongs are made from sliding from the
sound of one vowel to another within the same syllable.**

This page is effective for dictionary search to improve vocabulary.
The *eu* and *ew* sound like ue. Let's review why.

Try to say ēū quickly. The Roman letter v was pronounced ū. Romans had no letter u. Over time *"w"* was formed from two letters v which we name *"double u."* Now, *ew* says ēū ū. Say it fast. Remember to slide and glide the ēū fast or just say *oo* for ew.

"Wow! I never knew this history. I can do this!"

T Ask the students if there are any words of which they don't know the meaning.

Give some meanings. Look up some. Make this a **fast** and **fun** pronunciation activity. Dictionary work is like detective work, solving a mystery of unknown words.

1. **dew**
2. **feud**
3. **aircrew**
4. **view** (vēū)
5. **chew**
6. **chewable**
7. **Aleutian**
8. **neutral**
9. **ewer**
10. **Teutonic**
11. **deuce**
12. **yew**
13. **sinew**
14. **drew**
15. **mildew**
16. **curfew**
17. **lew**
18. **mew**
19. **grew**
20. **Lewis**
21. **feudal**
22. **neuron**
23. **hewn**
24. **dewdrop**
25. **strew**
26. **eschew**
27. **askew**
28. **new**
29. **Eūrope**
30. **eulogy**
31. **spew**
32. **stew**
33. **strew**
34. **euphony**
35. **askew**
36. **Newton**
37. **vacuum**
38. **steward**
39. **anew**
40. **EUREKA!**

* * * * * * * * *

Bonus: **pneumonia**

itis = inflamed
neuritis
tonsilitis

Whew! That was easy!

- **Sometimes you will meet nice people with silly names.**
- **Sometimes you will meet silly people with silly names.**
- **Read the sounds.**
- **Follow the rules!**

When in doubt, ask politely, "How do you pronounce your name?"

1. **I know Mr. Cheapfeat.**
2. **I saw Sam Stewseal.**
3. **Give a box to Mrs. Mildpeat.**

📖 ™ This last name could be pronounced with a long i – Mildpeat. It could also be pronounced with a short sound as in Mildpeat. Names can have different or unusal pronunciations.

The author of this phonics program pronounces her last name as DŌ-RAŃ with the accent on the last syllable. Other people with the same spelling may pronounce it DŌŔ –AN. It depends on what one prefers.

You might have to ask politely, "May I ask how you pronounce your name?" That is courteous and acceptable.

4. **That man is Quint Weaksqueak.**
5. **Call Mr. or Mrs. Trainerdrainer.**
6. **Open doors for Mr. Pewterpan.**

7. **Sit with Mr. or Mrs. Cruelpaint.**
8. **Look for Sue Sightmight.**
9. **Sell candy to Lewis Strewblue.**

The problem with spelling OW! Ouch!

That hurts! Remember: ow/ou are the "hurt sounds."

Spill coffee and you will say "Ow! Ow! Ow! Ow!"

bow	wow	cow	how	now
flower	shower	cower	mēow	crown
owl	brown	crowd	vowel	howl

How now brown cow?

The ow will often say the name of O, as in sō and nō. How will you know?

You will need context clues or the dictionary to know!

1. snow 2. show 3. throw 4. tow 5. bow
6. blow 7. stow 8. crow 9. glow 10. grow

Ou can also be pronounced as in ouch.

loud	mouth	found	cloud	*Old spelling keeps <u>b</u> in *doubt* from the original Latin word *du<u>b</u>ius*.
ouch	flour	around	flour	
pout	sound	about	shout	
sour	house	slouch	doubt*	

TROUBLEMAKER ALERT! Long words? Dictionaries help.

-OUS AT THE END OF A WORD JUST SAYS -OUS

1. fa·mous 2. ri·dic·u·lous 3. mi·rac·u·lous 4. fab·u·lous

5. in·stan·ta·ne·ous 6. mo·men·tous 7. dis·as·trous

Read these silly ow/ou sentences.

The ou/ow sounds usually make the "hurt" sounds.

"Ow! Ouch! That hurts!"

1. How now brown cow?

2. We tried to surround the couch and shout in the house to chase the owl.

3. We used a brown vowel "A" when we made the crown for the fabulous townhouse tower.

4. A crowd in the town saw the cloud in the shape of a flower.

(Apparently, the crowd in the town wasn't very busy!)

5. Arthur's talking pig shouted, "Ouch!" when the couch fell on his snout.

6. The town cow can "wow" the crowd. It is a problem. The town cow just sits on the couch in the house.

(This must be the same town as in #4.)

Before 1150 A.D., these Old English sounds were pronounced with the effect of gargling or clearing the throat. However, now *gh* makes the /f/ SOUND if it is alone.

It makes NO SOUND if it is followed by t. Maybe people didn't like gargling sounds in public. We could have gotten along without this team, but it stayed around to cause us many problems in spelling!

Think of them as a sneaky, troublemaker™ team. When you see them, draw a line through them on the paper or think it in your head.

LEAVE THEM __OUT__ WHEN YOU __READ__. PUT THEM __IN__ WHEN YOU __WRITE__.

Meet the silent gh™ team.

Written as –ght, the gh is silent. It says NOTHING!

bou~~gh~~t   thou~~gh~~t   brou~~gh~~t   fou~~gh~~t   sou~~gh~~t   tau~~gh~~t

gh Rules

1. aught and ought say *awt* as in bought
2. īght sounds like *īte* as in nīght
3. eigh says *ā* as in eight (8)

ri~~gh~~t	bought	straight	**BIG TROUBLEMAKER!**
pli~~gh~~t	fought	flight	**height**
might	sought	taught	
sight	fraught	light	→ **A written** spelling review is necessary.
fight	Dwight	slight	
tight	nought/	weight	Have practice time first.
ought	naught	freight	

★ At the END of a word, *gh* says the sound of / f /.

1. c⟨ou⟩gh / kawf /   2. r⟨ou⟩gh / ruf /   3. tough / tuf /

4. tr⟨ou⟩gh / trawf /   5. en⟨ou⟩gh /enuf/   6. laugh / laf /

CONFUSED? THIS TAKES PRACTICE, BUT IT PAYS OFF!

small  tall

The teams of <u>al</u>t, <u>al</u>k, <u>au</u>ght, <u>all</u>, <u>ou</u>ght sound like *aw / au* as in sm<u>all</u> and t<u>all</u>.

wall	gall	pall	malt	walk
all	stall	ball	halt	talk
mall	aloof	call	fault	stalk
tall	hall	fall	Walt	false

Some other *al* words are:

always   also   altogether   although   almighty

> ➔ READING AND SPELLING: Practice for *al* words.

T First have the students read the sentences. Then, dictate for spelling.

1. We can all meet in the hall after class.

2. Halt! Stop! You can't go there.

3. This is my friend, Walt. *Walt* is a nickname that is short for Walter.

4. I am going to take a walk with Walt and talk.

5. He will not balk at homework. He likes to do it.

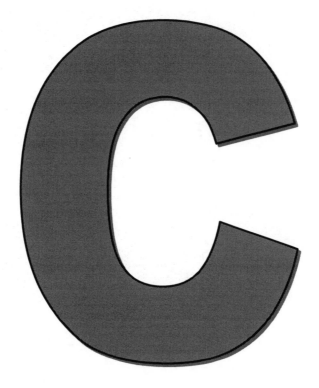

What sound does this letter make?

Answer: You cannot know for certain. It depends on the letter that follows it.

HERE IS THE LETTER C.

C

TOP SECRET! Most people do not know that you cannot tell what sound to make when you read a C until you know the letter that follows it!

Here is the secret: **When you are reading a word and you come to a C, quickly notice the very next letter. If you have a ce, ci, or cy, the C is pronounced / S /.**

c<u>e</u>nt	cement 	cypress
c<u>e</u>nter	cymbal	spice
cider	cellar	cinder
century	central	fleece
cinnamon	Ci<u>ce</u>ro	lucid
certain	censor	tacit
citizen	silence	incense
incite	license	vicinity
recital	placid	

REMEMBER: If you see ce, ci, or cy, C ALWAYS sounds like /S/.

Cute candy cane!

If a c is followed by any other letter—

(besides *e*, *i*, *y*)

—it says the / k / sound.

T To avoid confusion tell students that they have already learned the other exception. Briefly review ch, page 43.

ca**sh**	**c**ollar	**c**ollege	be**c**ause
cuff	s**c**urry	**c**oast	**c**old
opti**c**al	con**c**rete	**c**offee	con**c**lude
class	**c**ompact	con**c**ede	
ca**s**tle™	va**c**uum™		

→ Pronounce this *vac u um* to spell it correctly.

If C is the LAST LETTER in a word, say the / k / sound.
picni**c**   Pacifi**c**   specifi**c**   Atlanti**c**

TRY YOUR "C" SKILLS WITH THESE SENTENCES.

1. **We can scurry and have time for a cup of coffee.**

2. **I concede that, because you are in this class, you are a confident reader.**

3. **The compact car got stuck in the wet concrete.**

4. **In October, we went to visit a castle near the Atlantic Coast.**

This is a test to "c" how well you can read.

T This page may be reproduced for student practice. If you are using the overhead, students could write the number of each of the following words on a separate paper. Answers on next page.

For each word, write s or k for the sound of c in the word.

1. canvas _____
2. canoe _____
3. notice _____
4. concordance _/__/_
5. conference __/__
6. evacuate _____
7. arctic __/__
8. bacteria _____
9. cupid _____
10. curb _____

11. picnic __/__
12. cream _____
13. license _____
14. celebrity _____
15. comic __/__
16. acre _____
17. citadel _____
18. crescent __/__
19. crocodile __/__
20. pacify _____

How many did you get correct? ___ Was it terrific?
➜This is a great page to review for spelling practice.

This is a test to "c" how well you can read.

For each word, write _s_ or _k_ for the sound of _c_ in the word.

1. **canvas**	_k_			11. **picnic**	_k / k_
2. **canoe**	_k_			12. **cream**	_k_
3. **notice**	_s_			13. **license**	_s_
4. **concordance**	k / k /s			14. **celebrity**	_s_
5. **conference**	_k / s_			15. **comic**	_k / k_
6. **evacuate**	_k_			16. **acre**	_k_
7. **arctic**	_k / k_			17. **citadel**	_s_
8. **bacteria**	_k_			18. **crescent**	_k / s_
9. **cupid**	_k_			19. **crocodile**	_k / k_
10. **curb**	_k_			20. **pacify**	_s_

How many did you get correct? Was it terrific?

Preview and pre-study the words, noting any troublemakers.
Sample study hints: *acre* is pronounced _ācre_. Remember the <u>c</u>
and the <u>silent e</u>. Take note of the placement of <u>c</u> and <u>s</u> in
license.

If you make any errors, study why. **ALWAYS LEARN FROM MISTAKES**.

DOUBLE "C"

FOLLOW THE C RULES when you have two *c*'s together.

1. **The first <u>c</u> has the sound of /k/. That is because it is NOT followed by an *e, i,* or *y*.** It is followed by a *c*.

2. **Then, look to see what letter follows the *second c* and follow the C rule for the second c.** (Consider each c separately.) **The second c may have either an /s/ or /k/ sound.**

READ ACROSS. FOLLOW THE RULES. SAY THE SOUNDS.

The word **accent** is pronounced **ak – sent.**

k s

📖 **Pronounce the following words. Watch for the /k/ sound of the 1ˢᵗ <u>C</u>. Be careful. ALWAYS look to see which letter follows the 2ⁿᵈ <u>C</u>.**

1. ac<u>c</u>ent
2. ac<u>c</u>elerate
3. ac<u>c</u>ident
4. ac<u>c</u>ept
5. ac<u>c</u>eptance
6. ac<u>c</u>ess
7. ac<u>c</u>essible
8. ac<u>c</u>omplish
9. ac<u>c</u>ession
10. ec<u>c</u>entric
11. ac<u>c</u>rue
12. oc<u>c</u>ipital

The eccentric man had an accident because the car's phone accessory was not accessible. He looked under the seat while he was driving. He pushed the accelerator before he assessed the situation.
What do you think happened?

Vocabulary Hint

A<u>S</u> • SESS' and *A<u>C</u>' • CESS* have different pronunciations and meanings.

What sound does this letter make?

**Answer: You cannot know for certain.
It depends on the letter that follows it.**

What sound does a  make?

What sound does a G make – not what sound does a *giraffe* make!

Top Secret ! **Most people do not know that the g has special rules!**
→ **To know what sound that g should be,
you must look at the letter that comes after g.**

**The *e, i, y* rule is not as strict with the letter g as it is with the letter c.
Usually, for *ge, gi, gy*, the g says / j /. Sometimes, g breaks the rule.**

**In 1017 AD, the King of Denmark took over the throne of England
and for the next 25 years, Danish kings ruled England.**

Therefore, more than 1,400 places in England have Danish names like
Der*by*, Rug*by*, Grims*by (–b y* meaning *town*) and Al*thorp* and Lin*thorpe*
(*–thorpe* meaning *village*). The letter g mixed with other languages
around this time.

The language was *fluid*, like water, flowing out in different ways and
taking different forms, adjusting, *fitting in*.

**The English writer, Chaucer, often wrote *yive* for the
word *give*.** Influences of the many people from Scandinavian
(Danish) tribes caused changes when common people lived and
worked together with the Anglo-Saxons (the people from the
lands of England.) **Just as today, people picked up each
other's sound, words and meanings.**

Margaret M. Bryant, Modern English and Its Heritage, Macmillan Company, NY, 1962.

T **However, SOMETIMES *ge, gi* has the 'hard' sound of g as in *go*.**

**Because of changes over time, a FEW exceptions do not follow
the g–rule like the following: give, gift, giver, given, get,
giddy, begin, girl, and target.**

Can you think of others?

YOU CAN GET GOOD AT G'S THAT SAY / j / !
ge / gi / gy

ge

refūgee
gesture
gentleman
suggest
gentle
danger
ledge
generate
fringe
germ
Germany
cāgey
angel

T How is angle pronounced? Why?

gi

gin
gīant
gist
magic
margin
origin

charging
fūgitive
gigantic
fragile ℮-™
giblet
ginger
gingerbread
tragic
longitude
original
eligible
dirigible

Remember: *ia* and *iu* say *e-uh.*

Algeria
Belgium

gy

gym
gyp
lethargy
gymnasium
stingy
edgy

gypsy
gyrate
gyroscope
prodigy

→ When you must double g to make a blocker, **DO NOT change the second sound** – *buggy.* Keep the *base* word (or root word) g sound.

In this case, the base word, **bug**, is pronounced. The g in the gy keeps the g or */gum/* sound.

If **fog** is the root word, how do you pronounce foggy?

T SPELLING REVIEWS PROVIDE PRACTICE. **Have students review** trouble-makers **in words, for example, note the** *d* **in -edge.**

---

fidget   gadget
midget   ledge
hedge   wedge
sludge   badge

REVIEW OF G WORDS.

Golly Gee!!

📖 Check the line next to the words that have the / j / sound of the letter *g*. If you are using another paper, write the numbers 1-50. Next to each number, write a g or a j to indicate the sound of each g in the word. This page may be duplicated.

🛈 Correct the papers with the students. Remind them that a wise person learns from his/her mistakes and improves in the future. Then, have the students read the words.

1. __ gender	18. __ great™	35. __ regular
2. __ goose	19. __ grime	36. __ vagabond
3. __ gas	20. __ game	37. __ segment
4. __ gentle	21. __ gallon	38. __ manage
5. __ grand	22. _/_ engage	39. __ dragon
6. __ generate	23. _/_ garage	40. __ German
7. __ glass	24. __ vagrant	41. __ agent
8. __ gem	25. __ wagon	42. __ longitude
9. __ graft	26. __ magnet	43. __ legislate
10. __ grass	27. __ wedge	44. __ vegetable
11. __ gutter	28. __ August	45. __ pigeon
12. __ genuine	29. __ codger	46. __ emerge
13. __ grit	30. __ group	47. __ congenial
14. __ glory	31. _/_ George	48. __ insurgent
15. __ grimace	32. _/_ ginger	49. __ courage
16. __ gold	33. __ giraffe	50. __ gewgaw
17. __ grip	34. __ gelatin	# correct_____

Answer sheet for test on p. 69
Golly Gee!!

T Correct the papers with the students. Remind them that a wise person learns from his/her mistakes and improves in the future. Then, have students read the words.

1. J gender
2. G goose
3. G gas
4. J gentle
5. G grand
6. J generate
7. G glass
8. J gem
9. G graft
10. G grass
11. G gutter
12. J genuine
13. G grit
14. G glory
15. G grimace
16. G gold
17. G grip

18. G great ™
19. G grime
20. G game
21. G gallon
22. G /J engage
23. G / J garage
24. G vagrant
25. G wagon
26. G magnet
27. J wedge
28. G August
29. J codger
30. G group
31. J / J George
32. J / J ginger
33. J giraffe
34. J gelatin

35. G regular
36. G vagabond
37. G segment
38. J manage
39. G dragon
40. J German
41. J agent
42. J longitude
43. J legislate
44. J vegetable
45. J pigeon
46. J emerge
47. J congenial
48. J insurgent
49. J courage
50. J /G gewgaw

correct_____

Fill the sack with <u>ang, eng, ing, ong, ung</u>.

The **short vowel + n + throat /g/ are slid together, as though you are swallowing. The -ng sound is not pronounced as a hard, "guh" sound because the / n / slides into / g / and softens it.**

Here is a little history to help you to understand the –ng family. As ordinary people of old tribes got together, they picked up words from each other: Old English, Germanic words, Greek, French and Latin words were shared among peoples as they met.

To expand meanings, they would adapt their words with word parts like *ang, eng, ing, ong,* **and** *ung* **of other people they met. They also probably substituted the** *–ng* **sound for** *–nk* **sound.**

Modern English and Its Heritage, p.157.

→	**furh**	= Middle English's **furrow**
+	<u>**lang**</u>	= Anglo Saxon's <u>**long**</u>
	furlong	= Meaning: **length of a furrow** Now = 1/8 mi.
→	*Kyning + dom*	= Middle English's *kingdom*

📖 Practice: Into the <u>long</u> sack, please place a toy with a b<u>ang</u>, a p<u>ing</u>-p<u>ong</u> paddle, a g<u>ong</u>, a rock<u>ing</u> horse and seven r<u>ings</u>.

bang	**flinging**	**anger** ™/g/ as in go
clang	**jingle**	**congress**
hang	**flamingo**	**tangle**
rang	**thing**	**finger**
sang	**ring**	**stinger**
length	**string**	**ang<u>le</u>**
strength	**kingdom**	Remember *ang*™: angel
strengthen	**song**	.
bring	**gong**	
wing	**long**	**For words <u>starting</u> with GN and KN, the G and K letters were once pronounced, but now are silent:**
winging	**belong**	
sling	**strong**	
sing	**lung**	
singing	**tong**ue	ⓖnome ⓖnat
fling	**rung**	ⓖnaw Ⓚnee
		Ⓚnack Ⓚnap
		Ⓚnead

THE H COMBO: A trouble-making pretender!

The consonant h plays a very important role in reading. It showed up in many places as languages developed. Therefore, we see h teaming up to make many different sounds:

ch   gh   sh   wh   chr   ph   th

We may hear sounds pronounced as though they are written as *sh* or *zh* or *zsh*. They may have once been written as part of the word, but are not any longer. Perhaps people just slurred these sounds as they spoke.

They wrote as they thought they heard a sound just as someone today may misspell "*cando*" for *candle*.

In the words below, the **s** and **z** make the sound / *zsh* / as in the sentence,

"In this a<u>z</u>ure box is a trea<u>s</u>ure that will give me plea<u>s</u>ure."

Students can mark the troublemakers first before they read.

The dictionary is very helpful to use for reading and spelling these words.

1. plea<u>sure</u>
2. a<u>zure</u>
3. trea<u>sure</u>
4. collision
5. vision
6. exposure
7. composure
8. measure

9. decision
10. revision
11. osier
12. hosiery
13. glāzier
14. brā'sier
    brā'zier*
    (brā- *zsh*ure)

* Pronounced the same, meaning a *container to hold charcoal, fire.*

16. sei<u>zure</u>
    (see- zsh ure)
17. lei<u>s</u>ure
    (lee- zsh ure)

When you see these words, pay attention to troublemaker tricks so that you will spell them correctly.

→ Spelling practice is necessary for this lesson. Preview and pre-analyze words to be spelled. **Use a dictionary as needed.** 📋✏️

THE **tion / sion** / shun / TEAMS
with
cial / sial / tial / tious / cious

THIS WHOLE TEAM BREAKS THE RULES!

If a **ti**, **ci** , or **si** is followed by a vowel, it usually makes the /sh / sound:

op-**tion** = op- /shun/   pa-**tient** = pā-/shent/   cau-**tious**= cau-/shus/

T As we have seen, language and pronunciation change over the years. We write the letters, but we often slur them when we speak. We slide them so fast that the sound seems to change. Try saying the sounds, *t-ee-on* quickly 15 times. Listen to the slur. If you go very fast, it sounds something like *"shun."*

Top Secret!   BUT VERY, VERY IMPORTANT!!

→ When an *a* or *o* comes just before any *tion / sion* team member, an *a* or *o* usually **says its name**: ā-tion or ō-tion as in nā**tion** or nō**tion**.

As you read the words, follow all of the rules.
- **Do not guess!**
- Read each sound as it is written, left to right. If you are reading aloud, notice how your mouth shape changes as you read each sound across the word left to right.
- **Do not add or subtract sounds!**
ti, si, ci followed by a vowel = /sh /

1. **fiction**   Say: *fic•shon*
2. **addition**
         Say: *add•i•shon*
3. **mul·tip·licātion**
4. **division**
5. **nominātion**
6. **ac·cu·mu·lātion**
7. **par**[**tial**]
8. **substan**[**tial**]
9. **residential**
10. **explōsion**

REMEMBER: *ous* says /us/.

Read the sounds from left to right.

11. **infectious**
12. **repe·ti·tious**
13. **ambitious**
14. **delicious**
15. **nutritious**
16. **vorācious**
17. **conscious**
18. **unconscious**
19. **fictitious**
20. **vicious**
21. **grācious**

📖 **SPELLING REMINDER: Learn which words are spelled with si or ti or ci** : /sh/-sounding **troublemakers.** 📄🖊

MORE *TIONS* IN *MOTION!*

Read each consonant, vowel or vowel team's sound as you read across each word.
DO NOT GUESS.   DO NOT SKIP.   DO NOT ADD SOUNDS.

Follow the rules that you have learned.   You will probably make some *accommodation* (change) for your local *dialect* (accent).
USE CONTEXT TO UNDERSTAND MEANING OR USE A DICTIONARY.

1. **add · i · tion**   **nom · i · nā · tion**   **con · ven · tion**

There was an addition to the nomination list at the convention to elect a president.

2. **si · tu · ā · tion**   **for · mā · tion**   **con · sid · er · ā · tion**

After careful consideration, there was a formation of a group to study the situation.

3. **sen · sā · tion**   **fū · mi · gā · tion**   **ac · com · mo · dā · tion**

Because of the fumigation in the hotel to kill large insects, the burning <u>ch</u>emical sensation made the people sick. The hotel made other accommodations.

The use of a dictionary is required to clarify the pronunciation of a word.

4. **e · vap · or · ā · tion**   **pre · scrip · tion**   **spec · u · lā · tion**

There was speculation that the evaporation of some of the medicine made the prescription too weak to be effective.

"Pre" is a **pre**fix meaning "before." Say the long ē (tree) sound. "*Script*" means *write*. Therefore, a doctor WRITES a *pre-scrip*-tion BEFORE the patient can get medication.

Ṯ "Sight-readers" often confuse *pre* (meaning *before*) and *per* (meaning *through*). Students MUST read each sound *left to right* as it appears in the word.

ALL IN THE FAMILY PLAY ON THE SAME TEAM!
-tient / -cient sounds like / shent /!

Remember to read ti and ci as though they were written as /sh/.
Then, read the final sounds. Read: ti /sh/ + ent = / shent / and
ci /sh/ + ent = / shent /.

Learn which ™ /shent / endings begins with ci as in -cient, and
which begins with ti as in - tient. This will improve your spelling!

1. **patient** — My doctor took care of his **patient**.
2. **ancient**™ — **Ancient** history tells about events thousands of years ago. (Do you hear ãncient or ancient?)
3. **deficient** — My new, **deficient** TV didn't work.
4. **sufficient** — My $4.00 was not **sufficient** to buy a $5.00 book. My $4.00 was **in**sufficient to buy a $5.00 book.

> These are other members of the -ti™ team.
> These are written -tial /-sial /-cial but pronounced /shal /.
> **Keep a dictionary handy.**

5. **partial** — It was an incomplete order, only **partial**.
6. **confidential** — He could not see the **confidential** report.
7. **martial** — The words **martial** and marital are different.
8. **fãcial** — She looked at Joy's happy **facial** expression.
9. **palãtial** — The house was **palatial**, like a palace.
10. **rãcial** — It is good to see **racial** understanding.
11. **glãcial** — **Glacial** movement is like a slow ice river.
12. **nuptial** — A **nuptial** song was sung at the wedding.
13. **residential** — Ann's house is on a **residential** street.
14. **penitential** — **Penitential** means being sorry for a wrong.
15. **beneficial** — It is **beneficial** to brush your teeth.

Break down the big teams. Divide words into syllables.

Big words are *just like* small words joined in one word. Dividing words into *syllables* is like breaking apart the long word into little sections. *SYLLABICATION* (breaking into syllables) is based on pronunciation first. There are some rules to keep in mind.
NOT SURE? CONSULT A DICTIONARY. Dictionaries show how words are divided into syllables. On this page are some of the most common rules.

1. Two consonants **between** vowels: **v c cv**

USUALLY DIVIDE BETWEEN CONSONANTS. THESE ARE CALLED "CLOSED" SYLLABLES.

rab · bit   **mur · mur**   **fab · ric**   **mag · net**   **bar · ber**

2. One consonant **between** two vowels: **v c v**

Usually divide BEFORE the consonant.
IF THE VOWEL IS AT THE END OF A SYLLABLE, IT WILL SAY ITS NAME. THIS IS CALLED AN "OPEN" SYLLABLE.

sō · lō   **pū · pil**   **spī · ral**   **vē · tō**

3. Word ending in a consonant + le: **c + le**

mar · ble   **hur · dle**   **stum · ble**   **no · ble**
la · dle   **jun · gle**   **un · cle**

Exception: For ™ **troublemaker** words with

ackle / eckle / ickle / ockle / uckle, write the ck with the first syllable as in

pick · le   *tack · le*   *buck · le*   *knuck · le*

4. **- ed** is added to a word ending in /t/ or /d/
as in *-ted / -ded* words

The *–ed* is broken into a separate syllable: **rust · ed   twist · ed   wait · ed**

5. Usually, a suffix is its own syllable.

tall · est   **gold · en**   **golf · er**   **big · ger**   **beach · es**

6. Don't separate diphthongs into separate syllables.

oi - oy oil · ing / em · ployed	**ou - ow** out · ing / cow · er
aw - au law · yer / Au · gust	**ei - ie** de · ceive / be · lieve
eu - ew neu · ron / few · er	**ch** per · chance
	chr /kr/ Chris / chrys·al·is

Never separate a **gh / ph / sh / th / wh / ch / ng / qu**
USE THE DICTIONARY OFTEN!   It will tell you where syllables are separated.

Careful **PRACTICE MAKES**
~~PERFICT~~ ~~PERFICE~~ ~~PREFICT~~
PERFECT!

📖 ○ **Read these.** Note the troublemakers ™ sounds.
　 ○ **All of the words here are separated into syllables, as you would find in a dictionary, to help with pronunciation.**
　 ○ **Read and spell the sounds across** *left to right.*

con-ven-tion	stim-u-la-tion	mar-tial
con-sid-er-a-tion	leg-is-la-tion	fa-cial
rec-og-ni-tion	me-di-a-tion	pres-i-den-tial
im-po-si-tion	med-i-ta-tion	se-quen-tial
sit-u-a-tion	su-per-sti-tion	ev-i-den-tial
temp-ta-tion	ra-di-a-tion	pes-ti-len-tial
reg-u-la-tion	suc-ces-sion	con-fi-den-tial
e-vap-or-a-tion	in-ci-sion	cre-den-tial
spec-u-la-tion	ver-sion	
pre-scrip-tion	tel-e-vi-sion	[In the next word, *ien* says *ee-en*.]
e-val-u-a-tion	pro-vi-sion	ex-pe-di-en-tial
par-ti-ci-pa-tion	sub-mer-sion	spe-cial
sen-sa-tion	ad-he-sion	ra-cial
va-ca-tion	ses-sion	com-mer-cial
	par-tial	ex-is-ten-tial
		do-na-tion

oy/oi

It's *not* a dip song! It's a diphthong!

A **d i p h t h o n g** is a sound made from changing the mouth position to make one vowel sound slide into another vowel sound quickly and smoothly. They seem to make a new sound. Make your mouth say Ō. Quickly change shape to say i̱.

 **oil**

 **toy**

These vowel teams ALWAYS sound the same.

point	**soil**	**embroil**
poise	**soy**	**tabloid**
Remember: Final e's are silent.	**joint**	**loyalty**
broil	**joist**	**moist**
boil	**thyroid**	→ Most *oy* diphthongs come at the end of a word.
cloister	**Roy**	
doily	**destroy**	Preview and pre-study the words, noting any troublemakers.
foil	**employ**	
foist	**boisterous**	Spelling Study Hint!
hoist	**embroider**	Remember that *boisterous* has er.
Troy	**poinsettia**	
Joy / joy	**noise**	Take a test!
boy	**alloy**	
	coin	

You can take a bite out of hard words!

- Read letters across the word from *left to right*.
- Don't guess! Don't add letters or sounds.
- Pay attention to how words are spelled.

Use a dictionary to expand your vocabulary! It will also give you accent marks.

ā-e	specūlāte	invalidate	evaporate
ēe	draftēe	awardees	nominee
ē-e	compēte	complete	replete
ī-e	invīte	recite	divide
ō-e	antelōpe	antidote	implode
ū-e	exactitūde	aptitude	subterfuge

-a-	backpack not packpack	boomerang	fantastic
-e-	sentimental	negligence	pestilence
-i-	innerspring	insensible	civility
-o-	conglomerate	obligate	oncology
-u-	mistrust	unimportant	omnibus

a(r)	registrar Not same as register.	archery	arthropod
aw	awfully	drawback	pawpaw
oo	moonbeam	oology	roofer
oo	footstool	cookbook	lookout
ow Ouch!	coward	downstairs	lōwbrow

📖 **This addition cannot really be called a syllable**

because it is sometimes added to words *or* sometimes it just "blends in" with what goes before it.

Confused? When is the final *-ed* not a syllable?

Stick to the *–ted / -ded* rule and you will not come un-glued when you read or write <u>PAST-TENSE</u> verbs that end in *-ed*.

Stick to the following *–ted / -ded* rule.

1. **If –ed follows the letters *t* or *d*,** it is pronounced as *-ted* or *-ded* and is a separate ending.

Examples: *planted, raided*

2. **If *–ed* follows <u>any other letter</u>,** it is pronounced simply as / t / or / d /.

Examples: *harmed* pronounce as *harmd*,
ripped pronounced as *ripd*

⊤ The *d* may <u>sound</u> like a /t/ sound when you pronounce *ripped*, but try to pronounce correctly. <u>T</u> and <u>D</u> sounds are a <u>little</u> different. Pronounce *ripd*, not *ript*. Practice to enunciate correctly.

Top Secret! When you are writing and adding *–ed*, remind yourself that *–ed* acts just like the silent e at the end. If you do not want the vowel sound in the "root" word to change from short to long, you MUST double the consonant blockers just as in the word, ri<u>pp</u>ed.

PRACTICE STEPS to follow for correct –ed word pronunciation.

1. Underline the letter IN FRONT OF the final –ed.
2. First, go down the list and pronounce those words that have -ted/-ded as final syllables.*
3. Go back and read all of the other **non** -ted/-ded words.
4. Lastly, pronounce the entire list.

Think: "–ed acts like a final shadow e." Write *ripped*, **not** *riped*.

Top Secret! "-ing" acts like a final shadow E, too: ripping not riping.

1. counted
2. altered
3. depended
4. picked
5. stuffed
6. formed
7. stopped
8. waited
9. locked
10. faded
11. cashed
12. dented
13. braided
14. rushed

15. brushed
16. slanted
17. flopped
18. marked
19. bossed
20. cuffed
21. stressed
22. beaded
23. asked
24. compelled
25. tramped
26. played
27. scudded
28. rooted

29. destroyed
30. prided
31. kicked
32. invaded
33. cursed
34. prodded
35. gassed
36. bellōwed
37. tramped
38. benefited™
   Do not double the *t.*
39. cancelled
   Also spelled as canceled.
40. pretended
41. steamed

* Words with separate - *ted /-ded* endings are:
1,3,8,10, 12, 13, 16, 22,27,28,30,32,34,38,40

Notice spelling troublemakers.

IF YOU HAVE NOT PRACTICED ENOUGH, BE PREPARED TO PRACTICE MORE!

📖 Choose from the following words to complete the past-tense verbs in the sentences below. Double final consonants **if** you do not want to change vowel sound from short to long. Remember: final *-ed* acts like a **shadow e**. *The first answers are done for you.*

continue	~~believe~~	aid	~~gas~~	pass
permit	~~insist~~	arrest	rob	

1. The man ____*insisted*____ that he had not _____a stop sign without stopping.

2. The officer ____*believed*_____ him and _____ him to continue his trip.

3. We ____*gassed*____ up the car and _____our drive to visit a family. That family had _____us when our car caught on fire when we asked for help.

4. The man ____*robbed*____the bank but was _____.

ANSWERS: 1. insisted, passed   2. believed, permitted   3. gassed, continued, aided   4. robbed, arrested

→ The endings "*ed*" AND "*ing*" WANT TO BE LIKE ending SILENT *E*. You must include a blocker to keep the vowel *short*:

permi**tt**ing NOT permiting   ga**ss**ing NOT gasing   ro**bb**ing NOT robing
ru**nn**ing NOT runing   ho**pp**ing NOT hoping   si**tt**ing NOT siting

QU

The Romans borrowed the letter *Q* from the Greeks!
The sound in English is written *qu* and pronounced /qw/
as in *queen*. In English, the *q* is ALWAYS followed by *u*!
In some words, it has the sound of *k* as in the French
language. Thus, English phonetic pronunciation of Quebec is
kwih-BEHK, but the French pronunciation may be closer to **kay-BEHK.**
***Croquet* is *cro-kay*. *Iroquois* is Ir-o-kwoy.** (The final *s* is silent.)
The special highlights will help you study the spelling of these words.
Don't panic. When in doubt, **follow the rules** or **use a dictionary** for meaning or pronunciation.

These words have the / kw / sound.
1. **quack**
2. **quail**
3. **quit**
4. **quiet**
5. **quart**™ /qwort/
6. **queen**
7. **quick**
8. **quote**
9. **quill**
10. **quiver**
11. **quaint**
12. **quarrel**
13. **quality**
14. **question**
15. **quake**
16. **quantity**
17. **quarry**
18. **quad·ru·ped**
19. **equator**

20. **quintet**
21. **ēqual**
22. **square**
23. **squeal**
24. **squeeze**
25. **squall**
26. **squadron**
27. **sē·quence**
28. **sō·lil·ō·quy**
29. **Iroquois**
30. **equestrian**
31. **liquid**
32. **squash**
33. **sē·quel**
34. **squirrel**
35. **squelch**
36. **equip**
37. **frēquent**
38. **quadrille**
39. **sequin**

The following words have a final /k/ sound. They are borrowed from the French language.

40. **croquet**™ /kro·kay/

-*quette* says / ket /

41. **crōquette**
42. **etiquette**
43. **briquette**

-*que* just says / k /

45. **antique**
46. **oblique**
47. **catafalque**
48. **grōtesque**
49. **brusque**
50. **stat·ū·esque**

Qu Spelling Review for Page 83.

In the sentences below, some words are misspelled. Identify each error. Write the corrections on the lines after each sentence or on another paper. Remember:

   1. **Read the words exactly as they are written, *left to right.***
   2. **Pronounce correctly. Note any troublemaker sounds.**
   3. **Say the sounds exactly as you are writing, l*eft to right.***

1. **Sam is going to quite his job.**

_____

2. **Divide the pie into three equil parts.**

_____

3. **The quailty of the food at this restaurant is excellent.**

_____

4. **I ordered ten books, but the company sent the wrong quanity. They sent only two.**

_____

5. **There was much noise at the picnic. No one was quit.**

_____

Correct answers and always analyze errors!

1. quit → In the sentence above, there is a vowel team with a blocker. The word in the sentence says *quīte.*

2. equal → Notice the *al* spelling. Some mispronounce it as *il.*

3. qual*it*y → If you don't read each sound from *left to right,* you will make mistakes in reading and spelling.

4. quan*t*ity → If you don't read each sound from *left to right,* then you *will* make mistakes when you read and spell.

5. quī·et™ → In this ™word, the *quī* is an "open syllable." The *e* Is a short vowel. The *i* and *e* are not a vowel team.

The more that you learn
PREFIXES well,
the better you will read, write, and spell!

T Some early people knew only 1,000 words. *Old English* used ordinary words. People often added describing parts *in front of* words as *prefixes* or *in the back* as *suffixes*. As people encountered each other's languages, words were adopted and changed. The same happened to pronunciations. The expanding vocabulary grew and changed. Chaucer's CANTERBURY TALES, *The Wyf of Bathe,* below, is as an example of early English.

A modern translation after the arrow shows a change.

She was a worthy womman al her lyve. → She was a worthy woman all her life.

She hadde passed many a straunge streem → She had passed many a strong stream.

To Rome she hadde been… → **To Rome she** had **been…**   Modern English and Its Heritage. P.76.

Many words changed in use. For example, the word in Old English *"for"* meant, *"to destroy something."* We now only have a few words like <u>forget</u> and <u>forgive</u>. (What is destroyed? Anger?)   Sometimes Latin meanings were added to Old / Middle English words to make them clearer. Very many of the prefixes we use today come from Latin.

One of the important sources of Latin words came into everyday use because of Wycliffe's translations. Here are samples:

1. … *HE SAITH TO HYM*…   2. *I SHALL CUME*…   3. *HELE , HELID*
4. …*CENTURION ANSERINGE*… 5. …*ENTER VNDER MY ROOF*… 6. OONLY

MODERN ENGLISH AND ITS HERITAGE, P. 77.

CAN YOU FIND WORDS OF TODAY SUCH AS **HIM, COME, HEAL, HEALED, ANSWERING, SAID, ONLY, UNDER** ?

In the 1400s and 1500s, science and law introduced many Latin words. Numerous French and Latin words were borrowed and had begun to be used by many people. English became a richer language.

Words were borrowed from the Dutch or Germans as well as from other peoples. This added to the richness of the English language. You may want to learn more about English.

English lets people use a variety of levels of vocabularies. They can use just a simple vocabulary in a "popular style." They can be understood enough for them to "just get by" in life. This is limiting. On the other hand, YOU can become more knowledgeable and have an extensive vocabulary.   You will be ready to go anywhere, to meet anyone and to do anything in life!

STRIVE FOR EXCELLENCE IN YOUR SPEECH. IT WILL PAY OFF IN MANY WAYS.

T Latin is a "dead language," meaning it is not spoken as a native language any longer.   However, the study of it would add to your knowledge of and ability to use English more proficiently.   Latin roots live in the English language and Latin is still an important language to study.

YOU <u>CAN</u> READ WELL!

Count on prefixes to help you understand some big words!

- **A prefix is a syllable added at the beginning of a word to modify (*change*) its meaning.**
  - *Pre* means *before*.
  - **A *pre-fix* comes <u>in front</u> or is <u>*fixed onto*</u> the front.**

- **Many prefixes come from Latin meanings. (The more Latin you know, the larger your vocabulary can be.) This section gives you just some prefixes, but not all.**

- **Knowing the meaning of different prefixes will help you to determine the meaning of many new words.**

- **Try to learn the meaning of all of the prefixes on the following pages.**

- **Every time you learn a new prefix, review the old ones.**

- **Practice! Practice! Drill instills!**

- **Learn these and other prefixes. Your vocabulary will grow.**

PRE-VIEW PREFIXES

ad-	to
ante-	before
anti -	against
circum-	around
con-	with,
de-	down, from
dis-	apart
ex-	out
in-	in
in-	not
inter-	between, among
intra, intro-	within
mis-	wrong
per-	through
post-	after
pre-	before
pro-	before, for
re-	again, back
se-	aside
sub-	under
super (sur)	above
trans-	across
un-	not
uni-	one
bi-	two
tri-	three

ab = from

T UNABRIDGED dictionaries give most words and word origins and are very helpful. A few words have been selected to show how original meanings use prefixes.

1. **abnormal**
2. **abstract**
   Latin: *ab = from* Latin: *trahere = draw*
3. **abandon**
4. **abase**
5. **abrupt**
6. **abduct**
   Latin: *ab = from* Latin: *ductus = lead away*

---

6. **abstain**
7. **absent**
8. **abdicate**
9. **absolve**
10. **abolish**

📖 The next word, *avert* was *abvert*, but changed over the years.

11. **avert**

---

1. **adverb**
2. **advance**
3. **adhesive**
4. **admit**
5. **advocate**
6. **ad·jacent**
7. **addition**
8. **advantage**
9. **adjust**
10. **ad·jective**

ad = to

📖 The next ten words have lost the d over the years. Try saying them with the d.

11. **acquire**

📖 The letter after a has been doubled for these words.

12. **affix**
13. **aggressive**
14. **allude**
15. **annex**
16. **apply**
17. **arrest**
18. **assist**
19. **attract**
20. **asset**

ante = before

Hint: Both *ante* and *before* end in e.

1. antēbellum
   Latin: *ante = before,*
   Latin: *bellicus = warlike*
2. antēcedent
3. antērior
4. antenuptial
5. antechamber

6. antepenult
7. antediluvian
8. antemeridian*

* ante = *before*
meridian = *middle*

That is why we write a.m. **or** A. M. **in upper case, smaller letters for morning, that is,** *before* **the** *middle* **of the day.**

anti = against

Hint: Both anti and against have an i.

1. antīclimax
2. antīaircraft
3. antifreeze
4. antitoxin
5. antiseptic
6. antibiotic
7. an·ti´pathy
8. antidote

9. antilock
10. antibacterial

📖 Sometimes a hyphen is used with *anti-* as in the following words:

11. anti-arthritis
12. anti-tax
13. anti-knock

📖 When in doubt of meaning or spelling, consult a dictionary. **Review previous prefixes.**

circum = around

1. **circumnavigate**
2. **circumflex**
   Latin: *circum* = around
   Latin: *flectere* = bend
3. **circumspect**
4. **circumvent**
5. **circumference**
6. **circumscribe**
7. **circumstance**
8. **circumlocution**
9. **circus**

📖 The following words have origins <u>related</u> to *circum*

10. **circle**
11. **circular**
12. **circulate**
13. **circuit**

📖 **Review previous prefixes.**

> Reading, writing and spelling are easier when you comprehend more words.
> **Try these sentences!**

1. The arrested man had to **affix** his name to admit that he had **abducted** the president's dog during the **ante**bellum period. He was caught in the post-war time.

2. At 11 a.m., a Navy man entered the **ante**chamber of the command room. The captain of the ship was there. He commanded the ship that was **circum**navigating the world to fight against an alien enemy.

   Several **circ**ular alien **anti**-aircraft from outer space were shooting at the world's armies and trying to **ab**duct **ab**normal creatures from the **circ**us.

con

from Latin *conducere* meaning *to lead* =

with, to bring together

1. **contract**
2. **congeal**
3. **conform**
4. **congest**
5. **compress** *See #12.

6. **congregate**
7. **consolidate**
8. **concert**
9. **confide**
10. **concurrent**

The next words began the same, but the <u>n</u> has been dropped.

11. **collaborate**
12. **compress**
13. **correspond**
14. **co-operate**
15. **comprehend**

Sometimes con means against because it is shortened from *contra*. See below.

contra

from Latin *contra* - meaning *against* =

against

1. **contrary**
2. **contradict**
3. **contraction**
4. **contradiction**

de =
down,
from,
reverse
action

1. **de**clare
2. **de**scend
3. **de**hydrate
4. **de**compress
5. **de**form
6. **de**generate
7. **de**posit
8. **de**crease
9. **de**fault

dis =
apart

1. **dis**appear
2. **dis**claim
3. **dis**card
4. **dis**courage
5. **dis**trust

6. **dis**obey
7. **dis**tribute
8. **dis**miss
9. **dis**agree
10. **dis**respect

📖 The s̲ has been dropped for the following words:

11. **di**ffuse
12. **di**gress

The old man **de**flated the balloon after it appeared that the child **dis**carded it and went home.

The club rule is that members will be **dis**missed from the club and they must **de**part if they show **dis**respect to a mentor or the rest of the students.

ex = out
out of , outside of

1. exit
2. except
3. excel
4. explode
5. external
6. extend
7. export
8. expel

📖 The following words may have been written with the x, but the x was changed or dropped over the years.

9. eccentric
10. effervesce
11. emerge
12. emigrant

_____

📖 To emigrate means to go outside of a place. This means to leave.
To immigrate means to come into a place.

_____

Example:
The man emigrated from Spain and immigrated to England.

in =
in, put in

1. invade
2. invest
3. income
4. inhabit
5. inject
6. infection
7. induct
8. inspect
9. insert

in = not
sometimes has been substituted by
il, im, ir.

1. incorrect
2. invisible
3. inseparable
4. inappropriate
5. insoluble
6. indigest
7. insufficient
8. inept
9. ineligible
10. infirm
11. inactive
12. illegal
13. illiterate
14. immoral
15. impossible
16. immaterial
17. irresponsible
18. irreconcilable
19. irrational
20. irregular

Many words are very easy to comprehend by adding the prefix to the commonly known word. Students can look up some of the words that may be unknown.

What? The salesman's answers to the questions were inept and irrational. (The people bought the new car anyway.)

HUH? The irresponsible company exported invisible debugging equipment. (The bugs were happy!)

Sale! You can buy very inexpensive, irregular, deflating parachutes with insufficient emergency cords on sale! (Would you be interested?)

inter
=
between, among

Memory note: *inter* and *between* have an <u>e</u>.

📖 Always use a dictionary if you are unsure of syllabication or accents.

1. in·ter·act
2. in·ter·na·tion·al
3. in·ter·view
4. in·ter·vene
5. in·ter·face
6. in·ter·lock
7. in·ter·min·gle
8. in·ter·re·la·ted
9. in·ter·tri·bal
10. in·ter·ven·tion
11. in·ter·weave
12. in·ter·val
13. in·ter·change
14. in·ter·cept
15. in·ter·com

The word, *intercom*, is short for *intercommunication system.*

intra /
Pronounced "intruh"
intro =
within

1. **intramural**

   Latin: *murus* = walls,
   e.g. (for example), walls of a city, school

2. **intramuscular**
3. **intravenous**
4. **intracellular**
5. **intrastate**
6. **intracollegiate**
7. **intracardiac**
8. **intramundane**

9. **intrabox**

📝✏️ Review previous prefixes.

THIS PREFIX PAGE HAS BEEN MISMANAGED!

What do you think *mismanaged* means?

1. **misrepresent**
2. **misinform**
3. **m i s t A k e**

4. **mismanage**
5. **misjudge**
6. **misdeal**
7. **mmmmisspell**
8. **misbehave**
9. **misalign**
10. **mistreat**
11. **mislead**
12. **misdial**

mis = **wrong**

Did you find **mis**takes? #3, 7, 9

per = through

1. **percolator**	6. **perforate**
2. **permanent**	7. **perspire**
3. **persist**	8. **perceive**
4. **perennial**	9. **permē·āte**
5. **perspective**	10. **perforce**

Sometimes, we still use complete Latin phrases. *Per* is a Latin preposition meaning *THROUGH, BY MEANS OF, FOR EVERY....*

11. *per annum* - by the year, annually

12. *per capita* - for each person

13. *per diem* /dee-em/ - for each day, daily

14. *per se* /say/ - by itself, considered by itself

- Bob earned $50,000 *per annum*.

- The business spent $3,000 *per annum*, *per capita* for insurance.

- The mayor received $25 *per diem* for travel expenses.

- Cars are not bad *per se*. Bad drivers cause accidents.

pre = **before**

Remember this trick to remember the meaning:
P**RE** and BEFO**RE** both end in the letters **r** and **e**.

1. **pre**test
2. **pre**determine
3. **pre**possess
4. **pre**pare
5. **pre**amble

6. **pre**caution
7. **pre**requisite
8. **pre**view
9. **pre**dict
10. **pre**scribe

post = **after**

1. **post**graduate
2. **post**humous /pŏst hu mous /
3. **post**pone
4. **post**erity
5. **post** nuptial
6. **post**lude

7. **post**erior
8. **post** obit

9. **post** mortem
10. **post** date
11. **post**fix (suffix)

Post **M**eri**diem** = after the middle **of the day** - p.m. / P.M.

Post (after)   **S**cript (write)
P.S. - a note written as a thought after the signature.

T Frequently review and drill all of the prefixes that have been learned.

pro = for, before

- The wise **pro**fessor **pro**moted reading projects.
- The discussion gave the **pro**s and cons of the topic.

1. **produce**
2. **proclaim**
3. **proceed**
4. **protect**
5. **promote**

6. **protrude**
7. **profess**
8. **prospect**
9. **propose**
10. **project**

Optional spelling quiz.

MORE PRACTICE

- The man **pro**ceeded to write out a check to donate to charity.

- We had to **pro**tect the little lost puppies.

re =
again, back

Erase and re-do!
Use a hyphen to prevent confusion:
in **meanings** [**re**-form is not re**form**]
or awkward **spelling** [re-enlist not reenlist].

1. **re-do**
2. **retrace**
3. **return**
4. **repair**
5. **release**

6. **research**
7. **repeat**
8. **re-start**
9. **rēinstate**

10. **reprint**
11. **replace**
12. **retort**
13. **remīnd**
14. **rē·iterate**

15. **reply**
16. **refer**
17. **re-argue**
18. **report**

Optional spelling quiz.

se =
aside, apart

I selected this gift for you.

Not all words that begin with <u>se</u> have this meaning.
However, these next words are words that have their origins
and meanings related to <u>se</u> .

1. **secure**
2. **select**
3. **secret**
4. **seclude**

5. **sequester**
6. **separate**
7. **secretary**
8. **section**

sub = under, below

1. **submarine**
2. **substitute**
3. **subscribe**
4. **submerge**
5. **suburb**
6. **subdue**
7. **sublet**

8. **subscript**
9. **subordinate**

These are "*sub*" related words. <u>B</u> *was*
probably left out in the next words.

10. **succumb**
11. **suggest**
12. **support**
13. **suspect**

📖 Review previous prefixes.

super = above

- **The man has superhuman strength.**
- **He has super<u>ior</u> form.**
  (Troublemaker alert: *i* before *or* sounds like *eor*.)
- **His nickname is *Superman*.**

1. **superior**
2. **superlative**
3. **superflu<u>o</u>us**
4. **superficial**
5. **supersede**
6. **supernatural**
7. **superhuman**
8. **superman**
9. **superintend**
10. **superscript**

Throughout time, the Latin prefix *super* may have been shortened or changed to become the French *sur*.

11. <u>sur</u>pass   12. <u>sur</u>vive

trans = across, through, beyond

1. **transgress**
2. **transform**
3. **transit**
4. **transmit**
5. **transplant**
6. **translu<u>ce</u>nt**
7. **translate**
8. **transfusion**
9. **transfer**
10. **transm<u>i</u>grate**

un = not

This 🐰 is an <u>un</u>usual, ugly <u>un</u>-bunny!

1. **un**happy
2. **un**certain
3. **un**lucky
4. **un**cover
5. **un**bent
6. **un**make
7. **un**kind
8. **un**fortunate
9. **un**load

THE FOLLOWING PREFIXES ARE **ENUMERATED** (*NUMBERED*) **PREFIXES.** DICTIONARY WORK IS IMPORTANT TO FIND OUT HOW THE **ENUMERATED** (*NUMBERED*) PREFIX AFFECTS MEANING.

uni = 1
1. **uni**cycle
2. **uni**form
3. **uni**corn
4. **uni**ty
5. **Uni**ted States
6. **uni**lateral
7. **uni**lingual
8. **un**animous
9. **uni**son
10. **uni**versity
11. **uni**color

bi = 2
1. **bi**cycle
2. **bi**focal
3. **bi**ceps
4. **bi**nocular
5. **bi**·athlete
6. **bi**cameral
7. **bi**annual
8. **bi**lateral
9. **bi**color
10. **bi**weekly

tri = 3
1. **tri**cycle
2. **tri**pod
3. **tri**color
4. **tri**plet
5. **tri**·lateral
6. **tri**angle
7. **tri**lateral
8. **tri**-chromatic
9. **tri**cen-tennial
10. **tri**plicate

	PREFIX	MEANING	EXAMPLES
1.	**ambi-**	both, around	**ambidextrous, ambiguity**
2.	**amphi-**	both, around	**amphibian, amphitheater**
3.	**auto-**	self	**autobiography, automatic**
4.	**be -**	make	**befriend, become**
5.	**hetero-**	different	**hetero<u>nym</u>, hetero<u>chromatic</u>**
6.	**homo-**	same	**homo<u>nym</u>, homo<u>graph</u>**
7.	**meta-**	change	**metabolic, metamorphosis**
8.	**neo-**	new	**neonatal, neophyte**
9.	**para-**	almost	**paralegal, paramedic**
10.	**pseudo-**	false	**pseudonym, pseudopod**

Some Prefixes That SHOW *AMOUNT* or *EXTENT OF*

11.	**equi-**	equal	**equal, equator, equidistant**
12.	**hyper-**	excessive	**hyperactive, hypercritical**
13.	**is-**	equal	**isometric, isosceles**
14.	**multi-**	many, much	**multicolor, multifactual**
15.	**olig-**	few	**ol'·i·go·chrome, ol·ig·op'·ol·y**
16.	**out-**	surpass	**outbid, outclass, outlive**
17.	**pan-**	all	**pandemonium, Pandora**
18.	**poly-**	many	**polychrome, polyclinic**

To spell some tricky words, know these **TOP SECRET** rules.

- ◆ **Memorize:** Write **I** before **E** except after **C**!
- ◆ **Remember:** Write **I** before **E** except after **C**!
- ◆ **Always spell / write I** before **E** except after **C**!

GOT IT? GOOD! Now, try saying it with you eyes closed!

 cei says /see/.

1. **cei**ling   2. re**cei**ve   3. re**cei**pt   4. de**cei**ve

5. de**cei**t   6. con**cei**ve   7. per**cei**ve

📖 **Read these sentences. Practice spelling.**

ALWAYS USE A DICTIONARY TO LOOK UP MEANING OF UNKNOWN WORDS.

A. Do you have the re**cei**pt to show that you paid for the **cei**ling repair?

B. I find it difficult to con**cei**ve of the fact that he tried to de**cei**ve you.

C. Did you **perceive** that the false **receipt** was a **deceitful** way of getting out of paying the bill?

**How can you SPELL very TROUBLESOME TROUBLEMAKER teams?
EASY! PAY ATTENTION when you encounter them!**

**When you see the *ie* vowel team together in a word,
it SOMETIMES -- BUT NOT ALWAYS -- breaks the rules.**

THE FIRST VOWEL IS SILENT.
THE SECOND VOWEL IS THE TEAM TALKER.

If you are not sure, try the Team Talker Rule, the troublemaker way, or use a dictionary!

1. p**iē**ce	9. f**iē**ld	18. bel**ie**f
2. bel**iē**ve	10. ch**ie**f	19. gr**ie**f
3. p**iē**dmont	11. n**ie**ce	20. shr**ie**k
4. ach**iē**ve	12. ach**iē**ved	21. w**ie**ld
5. retr**iē**ve	13. th**ie**f	22. s**ie**ge
6. ach**iē**ver	14. gr**ie**ve	23. sh**ie**ld
7. th**iē**very	15 l**ie**n	→ Correct spelling is important. As you read, pay attention to how words are spelled.
8. gr**iē**ving	16. l**ie**ge /lēj/	
	17. rel**ie**f	

YOU HAVE COMPLETED THE PSRS PROGRAM!
Are you rel**ie**ved? You now have a sh**ie**ld of
reading information to protect you from ignorance.
Bel**ie**ve in yourself! Continue to learn more. Ach**ie**ve
great things. Be outstanding in your f**ie**ld of life and
enjoy a p**ie**ce of the p**ie** of success! GOOD LUCK!

Appendix

Page-by-Page Helpful Hints
for Pat Doran's
PHONICS STEPS TO READING SUCCESS

The basic directions are on each page of the program. **However, if you would like more suggestions, the practical hints in this page-by-page guide may help you as you go through the program. The tutoring and classroom versions are color coded. The black-and-white student version is intended to be a companion item for seat work and homework, used in conjunction with the color version. If you are teaching a student using the black-and-white version, you may encounter less success than with the full-color version.**

The PSRS Study Cards are helpful for review, practice, word-wall categories, vocabulary activities, activities for sentence and story building, as well as spelling practice.

If you need extra copies of any version, we respectfully request that you honor the authors' work and all copyright laws that apply to this program. Please, do not duplicate except pages for which permission is clearly given. Thank you.

PHONICS STEPS TO READING SUCCESS [PSRS] IS NOT A COMPLETE READING PROGRAM

Phonics instruction teaches the correspondence between speaking and spelling of words. The letter symbol/sound relationship is like a code. The written word is made up of individual sounds that are represented by symbols/letters. This is the Phonics Code of the English Language. Students who use the phonics code can decode the pronunciations of written words with accuracy. PSRS is a fast-paced program to teach students how to use the code to decode (read) by going from symbol to sound and encode (spell) by hearing the sound and writing the symbol. With the basic code mastered, readers can adjust or adapt for common or regional pronunciations as they read.

It is the direct, systematic presentation of phonics word-attack strategies taught in an intensive (concentrated) fashion. The instructional goal is to teach basic word-attack skills. This skill development is systematically layered, building one concept upon the other. Such skill mastery develops the automatic and accurate recognition of words. It takes the guesswork out of reading. Phonics mastery will enable the readers to use their mental energy for comprehension of what is being read. **Be aware that students' reading speed may slow down at first, but accuracy will increase.** With time and practice, speed and accuracy will increase even more. This program utilizes both the research-based approaches, synthetic blending of sounds and systematic instruction of phonics, as noted by the National Reading Panel in *Teaching Children to Live*, as the MOST EFFICIENT way to teach reading.

PROBLEMS WITH WORD FAMILIES, FAMILIAR WORD PARTS, AND GUESSING

Students may have had exposure to *some* phonics instruction. Not all "phonics" reading programs teach phonics in a systematic fashion. Students may not have been taught to blend all sounds left to right. Often, programs teach familiar word parts, "word-families," or endings of rhyming words as *whole units*. Students use word patterns such as s|at|, bl|end|, and l|unch| wherever they appear in a word in order to "figure out" what a word is. Thus, students may look for familiar words or word parts from right to left or middle to front then back. This may result in the *dyslexic* or misreading of words, for example *legislate* as *leg-is-late*, *toned* as *to-ned*. Confusion occurs. Comprehension is compromised.

Do not be surprised as you teach this program that you may notice that students are guessing at entire words or reading only a few letters then guessing at the rest. Note that students may be effectively using ineffective strategies, such as looking for those word-family whole units or familiar little words that appear in various positions in words. To reaffirm, it is best to teach that sounds are blended left to right, such as /s/a/t/ .... /b/ /l/ /e/ /n/ /d/.... /l/ /u/ /n/ /ch/. With reading practice of decodable text, the students will achieve an automaticity and fluency when they encounter these often-used patterns.

AID TO CORRECT REVERSALS AND OTHER ERROR-CAUSING STRATEGIES

Focusing strategies are helpful to counteract dyslexia symptoms and other error-causing strategies. When students learn the phonics concepts and use decoding strategies, they may continue to try to read the word as a whole. In that case, a focusing strategy is helpful. Either you or the student should use a finger or pen/pencil point as a guide under (or over) the letters, beginning with the first letter in each word. Gliding the pointer under each letter or "team" as each sound is pronounced from beginning to end, left to right can overcome whole-word visual confusion and many errors.

Caution: Do not have the student place the pointer over/under the *middle* of the word as this may have the student attempt to see the word as a whole.

EXCEPTIONS TO THE RULES AND ERROR-CAUSING SIGHT-WORDS

The English language is a phonetic language and not a pictograph or logograph language. Therefore, the number of words that are to be recognized by sight or as wholes by their shape or configuration should be extremely limited to those words that are highly irregular and do not follow the code. Look-say methods do not use the English Phonics Code because they incorporate a method that was developed to teach the deaf to read using the configurations of whole words. With look-say methods, teachers are encouraged to say the word and have the student repeat the word, assuming that, if the student is provided enough opportunities to look at and say a word, he or she will eventually be able to read it automatically.

Of course, some words are not pronounced according to the basics of the phonics code. Others are pronounced with regional or local differences, having evolved over many years. PSRS provides strategies to help the learner to identify which portions of the word do follow code rules. These portions, such as "ey" in 'th|ey|' are referred to as "troublemakers."

The English language vocabulary has upwards of 1,000,000 words. When students are subjected to time-consuming, tedious drill on hundreds of high-frequency *sight-words*, students are artificially hindered in their reading abilities and academic growth. Students with decoding or word-attack skills can read most of the upwards of 1,000,000 words in the English language. These phonics-skilled students can focus more time and energy on their vocabulary building. A larger vocabulary leads to improved comprehension.

CAPs: COMMONLY-ACCEPTED PRACTICES WITHOUT ANY VALIDATING RESEARCH

Look-say, sight-word, and high-frequency strategies are examples of commonly-accepted practices (CAPs) without validating research showing they are most effective. CAPs serve to "cap" student reading achievement. Often, reading programs inadvertently promote confusion. Students may be drilled to memorize words by their shapes, as whole units. Words like *up, down, out, in, if, are,* and *it* are decodable. On the other hand, students also are taught to use the phonics code to blend letters' sounds or "sound out" words from left to right. Students may become uncertain and often befuddled as to how to read. "Is this a word I decode or is this one of my sight-words? Is that word *is, if, in,* or *it*?"

This is like a child asking, "Should I pat my head and rub my belly or should I rub my head and pat my belly?" Is there one correct answer? If so, what is it? It sets up a mishmash of choices in the reader's brain and an increased chance of confusion and errors as the student is reading.

Another example of a CAP is when the teacher as a general practice reads texts and passages first to "model" how to read the material. Students generally will do echo-reading or choral reading, following the teacher's modeling of what the passage says. If students are not capable of individual, "cold" reading without prior practice, students may become comfortable as dependant readers. Benefit to reading and academic achievement may be minimal. Reading scores may languish at artificially low levels.

A different commonly-accepted practice has stronger readers paired with weaker readers so they can "help each other." Weak students do not help stronger students become even better readers. While social interaction is essential, it must not supersede academic achievement for *everyone*. The use of stronger students as tutors takes from their own academic growth. Strong students should focus on reaching their highest potential, not simply grade level, and not give up their own limited learning time to teach less-capable students. Conversely, weaker students' academic needs should be met by teachers or trained, adult volunteers. CAPs cap the academic and literacy advancement of all students.

LEARNING DISABILITY OR *MIS*-DIAGNOSIS?

Most individuals can learn to read using phonics. Students with generalized "learning disabilities" ordinarily can learn to read using phonics instruction. Often "learning disabilities" are diagnoses based on a student's inability to read well. A reading "disability" can be developed by ineffective instruction when students are not taught to use effective decoding strategies effectively. There are many formal diagnostic assessments available. One informal assessment simply is to listen to an individual read. Does the reader not know how to use all phonics concepts correctly? Note the types of errors made that do not follow the phonics rules. Does the reader confuse words like *it* and *if* or guess at words? It will give you a clue as to what is lacking or what was not taught correctly. It is crucial to avoid misdiagnosis.

PSRS uses systematic introduction of phonics concepts and synthetic (blending) strategies. With knowledge of the consonant sounds as a foundation, students are taught vowel concepts. Thus, students can blend the consonants with the vowel(s) to read across words, left to right, one single letter, vowel team, or digraph (*sh, th*) at a time. It is simple. Highly irregular words or parts are "troublemakers."

As you work with the student(s) to provide them with word-attack skills, encourage them to utilize these phonics strategies as they read throughout the day and refer to a dictionary when possible or necessary for spelling and for vocabulary development. The goal of reading education is to have all students become life-long, strong, *independent* readers. Be patient, positive, and encouraging. You and the students will experience real success.

SOUNDS

It is necessary that readers have what is called **phonemic awareness**, the ability to *hear* the separate sounds in words. PSRS reinforces that words are made of separate sounds.

CONSONANT SOUNDS: SAMPLE WORDS AND SUGGESTIONS

Teach consonants sounds *both* as beginning and final consonant sounds. Learners should be aware of sounds in words to know that words are made up of separate sounds. This helps learners grasp a better understanding of left-to-right decoding/encoding. Try not to teach sounds as /*buh* / or /*duh*/ but rather as / **b**uh / or / **d**uh /. The /uh/ is simply the breath of air needed to "push out" the consonant sound needed to pronounce the sound alone.

When we read words, the open-mouthed vowel sounds pronounced after a consonant /a/, /e/, /i/, /o/, and /u/ replaces the *breath* /uh/ needed. To read consonants, we will "blend" consonants into vowels, having the sounds *flow* smoothly from one to another. **Say** /b/ e/ d/ (bed) **not** /buh/ /ĕ/ /duh/ (**b**u**h**e**d**uh).

Note that when we say consonant sounds at the end of words, we do not hear the /uh/ sound: **t**u**b**, **p**lastic, **be**d, **t**uff, **h**ug, **p**ink, **h**ill, **ja**m, **p**in, **ju**mp, **c**ar, **c**ars, **h**ot, **wo**w, **f**ox, **b**uzz.

Bb	bed	
Cc	cat	• Teach the " hard" /k/ sound first. The c pronounced as /s/ is taught later in PSRS.
Dd	dog	
Ff	fish	
Gg	dog	
Hh	hat	• The h at the end of a word is usually silent. Therefore, using words *beginning* with h is the best way to teach the /h/ sound.
Jj	jump	• The letter j is not commonly found at the end of words.
Kk	key	
Ll	leaf	
Mm	money	
Nn	nail	
Pp	pig	
Qq	queen	• Teach qu as the /kw/ sound. In English, q is always followed by u. Also, in English the /kw/ sound is always spelled qu.
Rr	rabbit	• Teach this as the sound of r in *rrrrrrrrrip* or growl of a puppy. Do not teach the sound as /er/ or /ruh/.
Ss	sun	
Tt	top	
Vv	vase	• English words that end with a /v/ sound *usually* have a silent e at the end.
Xx	box	• Teach the x as the /ks/ sound, as in *fox* and *six*. Rarely, x at the beginning of a word has a /z/ sound as in xylophone or /eks/ as in x-ray.
Yy	yellow	• When y is at the beginning of a word, it says /yuh/.
Zz	zipper	

CHAPTER ONE - A-G

- Stress the important strategies on Page 113. You may want to post these to reference frequently as you go through the program with the students.
- As students read, be certain that all students are involved and that some are not pretending to read. Often, struggling readers can "hide" in choral reading, but with PSRS, when they apply the concepts, students will discover that they can read themselves.
- If a student has difficulty, have him or her use a mirror to aid in correct mouth formation.
- Older students must have an understanding of the value of the program. To help them, offer the following suggestions:
  - o Tell students that the reason they may struggle is they may have been taught to use ineffective strategies when they were first taught to read.
  - o Moreover, we now have studies that have been determined effective strategies for successful reading.
  - o In addition, this program is now being used in colleges to teach college students who may want to or need to improve their reading skills.
  - o The program is also being used to train teachers who may not have been taught how to teach explicit phonics.

Point out that if students struggle with reading, don't enjoy reading, are doing poorly in their classes because of comprehension problems, or are poor spellers, this program will help considerably.

Older students may complain that phonics is too babyish for them, but point out that PSRS is geared for older students. Nevertheless, tell your students that by *page C,* they will learn they can encode /read and *decode/spell without guessing* many 10- and 12-letter words they have never seen before. You may want to refer to Chapter 2, p.9. Students will have tools to accurately read and comprehend 15-letter words by using phonics and context clues.

Moreover, note that this program is used at the junior college level. You may also want to show students the large, college-level words in the prefix section beginning on p.84. Tell them that this program will enable them to read and spell those words. This will give students confidence and skill to enable them to read thousands of long scientific, legal, medical, business, and other unknown words that they may encounter throughout their lives so they will be prepared to read anything!

IT IS ESSENTIAL THAT THE STUDENTS HAVE A STRONG FOUNDATION UPON WHICH TO BUILD THE INFORMATION THAT FOLLOWS.

DO NOT SKIP ANY PAGES OR SECTIONS!

Students must pronounce all vowel sounds according to Page A. (You may want to keep this page out for reference. Enlarge it and post it, if necessary.) Refer to and stress the picture clues and the initial sounds. Have students pay attention to the shape of their mouth and position of their lips and tongue when pronouncing the vowel sounds. In this systematic program, "short vowels" are taught first; other vowel pronunciations will follow.

Tell students that the difference between the vowels and consonants is that vowels are pronounced with an open mouth. When one is pronouncing most consonant sounds, there is contact at various locations in the mouth (tongue, lips, throat, teeth, etc.).

Students may want to pronounce the "short" a as /ah/ in the word "want." However, make sure they pronounce the *a* as in the word "apple."

NOTE: Many English words that begin with the letters <u>wa</u> require that the reader say "woh" as in *want* (/wont/). That is because of the development of the English pronunciation and local regional dialects through the centuries and around the world. On the other hand, some <u>wa</u> words such as *wag* and *wagon* require that the <u>a</u> be pronounced as the <u>a</u> in *apple*. Local usage will dictate. Have students consult a dictionary whenever they have a question regarding standard pronunciations.

Because fast-paced PSRS is a phonics, word-attack program and not a complete reading program, it is better to go through the entire program first, if possible, before you bring in other reading tasks. As a result, they will be able to decode most reading tasks with accuracy. If this is not possible, you may teach the program daily for 30 or 45 minutes and/or throughout the day in 5, 10, or 15-minute segments. The format of PSRS allows for flexibility in instruction. Your goal should be to get the student(s) through the program as quickly as possible.

English-speaking students can make adjustments to their local, regional dialects for familiar words or use a dictionary for an unfamiliar word. English learners can use their dual language dictionaries.

 # Teach this program <u>as it is written.</u>

*What **NOT** to do:*

Do not give non-PSRS extra practice such "word families" like *–at* words, *bat, sat, hat.*
This can cause memorization by word configuration that can lead to reading/spelling confusion later on. Students may focus at the end of the word first. It may encourage students incorrectly to read from end to front, right to left.

Teach students always to "sound out" each sound from left to right.

- Do not have students look for little words or familiar words within a word to try to "figure out" what the word says.

- Do not break words into syllables for students. Let them pronounce sounds from left to right.

- Do not give clues such as, "It rhymes with…."

- Do not omit written spelling quizzes. These quizzes reinforce sound/symbol awareness.

- Compliment successes. However, if a student makes an error, provide instructional feedback:
    o "Read what you wrote exactly as you wrote it."
    o "What word did I say?" "I said, "_____." "
    o What do you have to change in your word to have it read (or say) _____?"
  . If the student cannot correct it, you have an opportunity to re-teach.

READ
LEFT  to RIGHT

Poster may be duplicated.

1. **When you read words, read across** left ➜ to ➜ right.
2. **Read each sound** left➜to➜ right.
3. **Do not skip any letters.**
   Use a pointer under each letter to help you read every letter.
4. **Do not guess.**
5. **Say each sound clearly and carefully.**
6. **Pay attention to the spelling of words as you read.**
   Look for troublemakers.
7. **Combine reading with spelling awareness.**
   Use a dictionary.

You will be more confident when you write.

CHAPTER 2

PROCEDURES FOR READING LISTS ALOUD

Make sure students read the word all the way through. **The last letter is just as important as the first.** Students are to be reading the words, sounding them out. Do not use teacher-student echo-reading or *parrot-reading.*

Teachers may be the guides, but they are not to read the words and have the students repeat the words. Students must develop *independent* mastery by using the sound-symbol relationships to decode each sound from first to last, from beginning to end. While there is some value in echo-reading or recitation, it must not be confused with independent decoding or reading.

If the student(s) mispronounces the vowel sound, you may review the sound using Page A or by modeling the sound. Use this as a "teachable moment." When teaching in a small or large group, it is *not* necessary to point out the student who made the error. The error itself is only needed for the teachable moment. When correcting the student(s), you can do the following:

- **Slowly** read the word from left to right **enunciating the sounds clearly** so they can hear and notice the difference.
- Have a **student** identify the error and then correctly read the word from left to right.

Initially, this will take a little time. Once the procedure is learned, this important step should only take a few moments.

Accurate decoding or *sounding out* is essential for accurate reading. However, it is also essential that the reader understands the meaning of the words in the sentence. Therefore, vocabulary development is most important and this program can be another effective tool for vocabulary development.

VOCABULARY DEVELOPMENT

After your students have read the words in the lists, ask them if there are any words of which they do not know the meaning. Select a few only. You may quickly give the definition to the class, use the word in a sentence, or perhaps, look up a word in a dictionary.

►Depending on time and circumstances, briefly discuss the meanings of only a *few* words.

Keep the lessons moving quickly! To use an analogy from this photo, think of the *Phonics Steps to Reading Success* program as the "emergency room of literacy." You must quickly "stop the *bleeding*" before you begin the therapy. In other words, stop the use of inaccurate and inefficient word-attack strategies before you begin focusing on other skills such as syllabication and comprehension. After you have gone through the program, you can return for review. With most students, you may have only a small window of opportunity to help, so you must move quickly.

Perhaps, put words on a vocabulary list or vocabulary "word wall" to be looked up later as part of vocabulary development. Your vocabulary word walls also may have categories related to the phonics concepts such as "Words with the AY Team." You may want to order the PSRS Study Cards to use with your word walls. See www.edu-steps.com.

SPELLING QUIZ PROCEDURE

Throughout the entire program, you will be expected to give a WRITTEN spelling quiz for most lessons. **Instructors who omit this activity have noted that their students are not as successful as those who have had spelling instruction and practice.**

Look for the PSRS spelling-quiz symbol: 📓✏️.

⇨ Both decoding (**reading**) and encoding (**spelling**) are essential skills for literacy success.

Choose 3-5-8-10 words from the page or list of words. (If you see that the students have grasped the ability to encode 3 or 5 words, it is not necessary to give more. However, if they seem to struggle with 3-5 words, stop, review the concept, pre-view the words, and give 3-5 more to reinforce the accurate spelling.)

- These quizzes are not to "trick" the students. Rather, they are included to help students learn to spell, left to right. Note that PSRS is primarily a decoding or word-attack program to help with reading.
- Because many words in English "break the rules," learning to spell accurately often requires <u>more study</u> and <u>practice</u> than does decoding. Encoding requires that the student hear a sound and recall the letter(s) that are used to make that sound. There may be several from which to choose such as *ea, ee, or ie.* This requires effort and/or study.

PROCEDURE

PSRS books have a spelling journal included in the back of the program, along with a vocabulary journal and the phonics rules aligned with PSRS. These may be duplicated. Students may use a formal spelling journal or any piece of paper.

- When giving the spelling word, slowly pronounce the word from left to right enunciating the sounds clearly.
- You may exaggerate the sounds if necessary since you are teaching the student to learn to use the sound/spelling relationship and not to memorize the letters in the word.
- Have the students watch your mouth as you form the sounds in each word, modeling each phoneme clearly.
- You may also use it in a sentence.
- Repeat words several times if necessary.

Have students say the sounds *aloud* <u>as they write each sound</u>.

For students who may have difficulty, take the following steps:

Review the concept that you are using, for example, say, "Look at the words we are using. All of the words will have the vowel team, *ea*, in them."

Look at *bread*, *head*, and *thread*. These words break the vowel-team rule. When you hear / e /, what should you write? (Answer: *ea*)

> You may preview and pre-analyze the actual words that you are going to give to the student.

Have students identify the words that they think might them spelling trouble. Help the student to pre-analyze the spelling of words you "might" give on the test, noting the phonics concepts that apply as well as the *troublemakers.* Be certain that the student is not attempting to memorize the configuration of the word.

Then, say the word, and have the student say the word's sounds **with** you (not after you) as you pronounce the word, one sound at a time, for example, say s—t—r—ea—m, as the <u>student pronounces and writes</u> s-t-r-ea-m.

· The student should be encouraged to pronounce the word aloud, slowly as he writes.
· See page 5 (#1, 2, and 3) of PSRS for demonstration of saying sounds and thinking about the concept or *troublemakers* as one writes.

After the words have been written, reveal the words to the student(s) and have the student(s) self correct their words. Let the students correct their own work. However, you generally should oversee the corrections. Some students may want to "hide" their mistakes or pretend that they did not make any.

Explain that they should not be concerned if they make errors, but that they can learn from their mistakes. This is a quiz to help them find out if and where they need improvement.

Analyzing Spelling Errors

Ask the student(s) if they made any errors in their spelling. If you are teaching small or large groups, ask the students if anyone would like to volunteer to share their error so that others may learn from it. A positive, safe learning environment is helpful for all. Always give praise to the students who share their errors. You want that student and other students to volunteer again in the future.

Example: "Thank you for having the courage to share your error," or "Thank you for having the courage to share your error so that others may learn." Or, you may give a "one-clap compliment," and say, "Thank you for having the courage to share...."

Note: Do not encourage applause, because all too often, the applause continues by one or two students, drawing attention to them and away from the student whom you are praising.

In analyzing spelling errors, have student(s) read the word, using the rules that they have learned, as it is spelled with the errors. In their vocalizing of the incorrectly spelled word, students will focus on their own writing. It will teach students to become more accurate and independent spellers.

For example: If the student spelled the word *mop* as *map*, have the student read the word as he/she wrote it using the phonics rules to pronounce the words.

· Ask the student how *map* should be written to have the *apple /a/* sound.
· Reading a word as written, according to phonics rules, teaches students to self-correct.
· Give the students the opportunity to correct their mistakes.
· Ask what is needed to correctly spell the word.

Do this for as many words as necessary. At first, it will take a little more time, but as you and the student(s) learn the process, it will take less time.

- If you see that the student(s) can spell three or five words without difficulty, do not to give more words. In that case, have the student(s) correct their work and then continue with the next column or page.
- However, if the student(s) encounter spelling [encoding] difficulty, analyze the spelling errors, and then, review the concept, preview and give three or four more words with the same concept.
- Correct and analyze errors.

Helpful Hints for Pages 1 – 104

Any information following the "T" symbol or T̄ is a "Teacher's Note." This means that it is information for the teacher. However, when appropriate to age or circumstance, the teacher may choose to read or relate teacher-note information to the students.

Page 1

Ask the students what sound the vowel makes before reading each list of words. Depending on the level of the student(s), you may choose to have a spelling quiz after each list or after the entire page is read. Follow spelling quiz procedure.

Page 2

Now that students have experience with the short vowel sounds, have the student(s) read the lists of words.

When instructing a small or large group, this is an excellent time to have each student take a turn reading a   word until the end of the list. You could also have the students read 'round robin' (one at a time) as well as do choral reading, that is, in unison. (When doing choral reading, be certain that each student is actually   reading and not just moving his/her mouth.) If you are working with only one student, sometimes, but not always, take turns so that the student doesn't get too tired. However, remember the analogy about learning   to drive that was discussed in the Preface. Follow procedures for reading aloud and spelling quiz.

Page 3

Stories may be read by student(s).

Do not have the student merely give an answer, as he/she may just be guessing. Have the student answer the question, but also find the sentence in the passage that gives that information.

Page 4

This page may cause some trouble but not because it is too difficult.

When you come to the _uck_-ending words, some students' lack of maturity will surface because of a common vulgar word with the same ending.

You may use an instructional hand gesture as follows:

Raise your open hand, with palm faced up, as you say, "Raise your standards," or "I expect more of you."

You also may want to use a quote from _My Steps Character Education Journal_: _"Foolish persons announce that they are foolish by their actions and words. Wise persons announce that they are wise by their words and actions."_ Pat Doran's _My Steps Journal, #16, Edu-Steps, Inc._

There are no spelling quizzes for this page until after you teach page 5. Review Spelling Quiz Procedure.

Page 5

This page is self-explanatory. After page 5 instruction is completed, you may want to give a few more spelling words from page 4 as needed. As you go through the program, continue to give positive reinforcement.

Page 6

Do not count a word as being wrong if the reader self-corrects. The error/correction will be adjusted with the added time the correction takes. Remind students they are trying to decrease their time and increase the number correct.

Discuss errors. For example, if student says *tack* instead *tick*, review left-to-right decoding. Also, some students who have been drilled on initial consonant blends may read *track* instead of *tack.* Focus the students' attention to reading all sounds, left to right.

Page 7

This page explains to students why they may be bad spellers and what they can do to become better spellers. Many times, students think it is their fault they are such "bad spellers."

Explain to them it is not their fault. Perhaps they were taught incorrectly. Add that if they follow this program then they will become better spellers. Students will no longer have to guess or think of the way the word looks in their mind.

Page 8

Reinforce the "le" rule by having students explain the rule or reading the rule first, then explaining it.

Page 9

Do not allow students to leave out any sounds when reading the pretend long words.

- Point out to students that they make the different consonant and vowel sounds by changing the shape of their mouth.
- If needed, refer to the short vowel Page A if students have trouble with any of the short vowel sounds.
- Remind students about having two consonants before the "le" when they hear the vowel's short sound. Teachers must not say the word first and have the student repeat!
- Use the teacher notes to prompt students to use context clues to find the meaning of a word. This will help their comprehension.
- Teaching the use of context clues for text comprehension is not the same as using context clues to "figure out" how to pronounce a word. (This latter use of context clues is an ineffective technique and reinforces guessing and inaccurate reading.)

Pages 10, 11, 12

In working with older students, as a class or individually, consider presenting in either of two ways, depending on your situation. The first option is to read "The Team Talker Vowel Story." The second option is to relate the concepts of the story. However, it is very important not to omit any of the concepts.

First Option: You may want to note the following possibilities:

- You may read the story aloud yourself to the student(s).
- If a student is a capable reader who is balking at the seemingly basic level of the program, you may want to provide some positive attention. Ask him/her to read the story aloud.
- You may ask for a volunteer to read it aloud, but make sure it is a student who can read well.
- Utilize a dramatization format.

Whoever reads the story, you should have all students silently follow along on the overhead, screen, or book with the reader as you move a pointer along, having them follow. Even if the students cannot read the words, you will be reinforcing the left-to-right strategy.

Second Option: To relate the story, you should read the story in advance and give all important concepts of the story. If it will help, you may want to write down the important concepts so you do not miss any points.

Page 13

Read this page to the students. Be certain that students understand these concepts as they will need to apply them throughout the rest of the program, specifically pages 14-19.

The directions for marking the *team talker* may help students who need to give themselves a visual clue to assist their decoding. It will also help them to become familiar with the diacritical mark that indicates the "long sound," that is, *name*, of a vowel.

Pages 14 - 23

The lessons on these pages use scaffolding strategies. This means each lesson breaks down the words for ease of reading, and then gradually uses fewer decoding clues to assist the reader.

The *scaffolding* used in the program lessons starts with a section of words highlighted in gray. These words are color coded, and have the long vowel *diacritical* mark. This is the mark found in the dictionary to indicate a special pronunciation. The words are segmented into phonemes (sounds) that can be easily *decoded* by applying the concept just learned. Then, each word immediately is followed by the same word to be read faster with fluency. (The section of words not highlighted may appear with modified pronunciation aids, such a *macron* (the long mark over a vowel to remind the student to say the vowel's name, as in the $\bar{e}$ in b$\bar{e}$am).

The final section does not use any pronunciation aids and is similar to text found in any print medium. After each concept or page, it is important to give a 3, 5, 8, or 10 word spelling quiz. Do not skip the spelling quiz. It is an <u>essential</u> element in the mastering of the skill.

As was mentioned in an earlier section, reading (decoding) and spelling (encoding) go hand in hand as students learn the sound/spelling relationships in the English language. You want the student(s) to be both good reader(s) and good speller(s).

Page 14

Remember to read or relate all the informational text on each page.

- The first $\boxed{T}$ gives the reason why some vowel teams do not follow the rules. For example, the vowels in the word *bread* are pronounced with the short *e* sound, such as in the word *bed* and not the long *e* sound as in the word *treat*.
- The next $\boxed{T}$ note gives a trick to teaching the spelling of words such as *creature* and *feature*.
- Do not forget the spelling quiz. You may pre-analyze the selected words. You want the student to understand how to focus on sounds and exceptions, but not to memorize the configuration of words.

Page 15

The program stresses the following strategies:

- Read across from left to right.
- Read each sound.
- Do not skip any letters.
- Let the letters be in charge.
- No guessing!

Please frequently remind students of these strategies.

Be patient and positive. Old habits are hard to change.

[Final note on p.15 addresses something that may confuse the students, perhaps because of something they may have seen in a pirate movie or cartoons. However, the only time *ay* is pronounced as a *long i* is in the word *aye* as in, "The pirate said, 'Aye, aye, Captain.'"]

Page 16

Help students to use the color coding and diacritical marks when reading.

The dots indicate which letters are pronounced. Use dots or develop your own symbols to assist students in pronouncing the sounds while reading from left to right.

To build vocabulary and to keep the lessons moving, ask students if there are any words to which they do not know the definition.

If there is more than one word in question, quickly give the meanings to the words and use each in a sentence, then move on. Perhaps, if there is a word of which *you* do not know the meaning, use this opportunity to model dictionary skills.

Again, however, **keep the lessons moving at a quick pace**. However, do not rush through by reading the words and having the students repeat after you or by skipping the spelling quizzes. Once the program is completed, you can return to do vocabulary development, if you desire to do so.

Remember to give spelling practice when you see the paper-and-pencil symbol. As you give the spelling quiz, enunciate the words very clearly and slowly. The student(s) may say the sounds aloud as they write. Remind students to think about which vowel of the vowel team is the silent vowel.

As they write the sounds that they hear from left to right, they must remember to include that silent shadow teammate.

In a Classroom Setting:

After the quiz is complete, ask for a show of hands to indicate which students spelled all the words correctly. Give praise. Then ask students in the class to volunteer to share any of their misspellings.
As mentioned earlier, remember to do the following:

· Give the volunteer praise for having the courage to share his or her error so that others may learn as well.
· Write the misspelled word on the overhead, board, etc.
· Pronounce the word as the student misspelled it.
· Analyze and discuss the misspelling, giving the person who volunteered the first opportunity to correct any errors.

In a Tutoring Setting:

After the quiz is complete, give praise for correct answers and compliment students who received 100 percent.

· Analyze and discuss the errors. Always give students the opportunity to make their own correction.
· Most of the time, they know how to correct their own error.

This procedure is extremely relevant in the development of proof reading skills. This gives students the skills to do independent spelling analysis and self-correction. They will know why a word does not "look right." Encourage them to become active readers, noticing how words are spelled.

Page 17

Bring special attention to the word *Braille* in the third column. This word may cause some students problems. One way students can remember how to spell words that might cause them problems is to first write the sounds that they hear in the order in which they hear them.

· They should make special note of the silent vowels and other letters that cause spelling problems. For example, the sounds that are heard in the word B*raille* are / brāl /.
  You may pre-analyze this word as follows:
  Instead of memorizing all 7 letters and their order, explain to students that for this word they have to remember to include 3 letters that are written but not pronounced.
· Students have to remember the silent shadow teammate *i* in the *ai* vowel team. They also have to remember the second *l* and the silent *e* at the end.

Students can approach any spelling word in this manner by making a mental note of silent letters or troublemakers. Students will then practice the short *a* and the *ai* vowel team when they appear in the final column. This reinforces the two basic phonics concepts just learned:

· A vowel by itself says its short sound.
· When two vowels are together, the first vowel in a vowel team says its name and the second vowel is silent.

Discuss with the student that just one thin vowel can change the entire pronunciation and meaning of a word. Note the following examples:

The artist didn't have his *pants* with him.   The artist didn't have his *paints* with him.

Point out how one thin vowel can change the entire meaning of a sentence.

Page 18

As mentioned on each page, remind students to use the color coding and diacritical marks for assistance. For some students it will be necessary to:

(a) Underline the vowel team;

(b) Cross out the silent shadow teammate; and

(c) Put the long diacritical mark over the vowel that says its name as shown on page 18.

Students learn differently. Some will comprehend the vowel concepts by merely reading, while others will require additional explanation. Still others will not master the concept without extensive tactile/visual reinforcement.

 **NOTE OF CAUTION:**

Do not be surprised if students sometimes continue to read the first few letters and guess at the rest of the word. Also, students may be able to correctly read big words, but get confused on "sight words." The teacher must be patient as old habits die hard. Do not, however, let errors pass without correction! Make corrections in a positive manner.

Encourage students to "Let the vowels be in charge. It is their game!" Follow *their* rules.

The *ie* vowel team has some exceptions. The T explains that the *ie* at the end of a word is a troublemaker because it says "ee". [See note at bottom of second column.]

Page 19

The *ue, ui*, and *ew* can pose a challenge to some due to dialect variations among English speakers. In the United States, these vowel combinations are not usually pronounced as the vowel's letter name of *u*. We pronounce them with more of an *oo* pronunciation as in the word, *boo*.

On the other hand, people from other English speaking countries may pronounce these vowel combinations as the vowel's letter name. For example, generally in the U.S. we might say, "That man has a *blooo sooot*."

However, in places in England, perhaps some might say, "The man has a blūe sūit," clearly saying the name of the vowel *u*.

Usually vowel teams are part of one syllable.

In some dialect variations in which the *ue* vowel team is separated into separate syllables, the vowels are also sounded separately. For example, the word *duel* can be pronounced as two syllables.

The syllables are separated between the vowels. Therefore, in some dialect varieties, the *u* is pronounced as a long vowel and the *e* is pronounced as a short vowel.

Many students may wonder why the *ew* is categorized with these vowel teams when the w is not even a vowel. The reason is that the w is a *double u.* (The u was written as a v by the Romans in their Latin language, thus double v = w.)

You may want to have your students look in an unabridged dictionary to learn more about the evolution of the letters/symbols over the centuries.

Page 20

In addition to the *ue* team, the *oe* may also be pronounced in separate syllables as in the words *Zoe* and *poet*, in various dialects or preferences. In the Name *Zoe* the *o* and the *e* are sometimes both pronounced as long vowels. In the word *poet*, the *o* is long and the *e* is short.

Column three gives a bit of trivia. Column four is important for reading and spelling. As the students read the list, make sure they note specific vowel teams used.

Also, note words like *meat* and *meet* may sound the same, but have different meanings. These are called homonyms from the Latin origins: *homo*= same; *nym* = name.

Remind students that they have to be alert as they read to understand word meanings and text.

Page 21

The *ae* vowel team is the least common; however, it still follows the rule. Though these words may appear to be more difficult, the students will read these words with ease if they just follow the rules. Make sure to give a spelling test after completing the first column.

Although these words are not common, they are easy to spell and will help build spelling confidence in your students.

Draw attention to capital letters. Remind students to use lower case letters, except when writing names and the first letter of a sentence.

As always, compliment successes. Analyze and correct errors.

For the second and third column focus on practice with all vowel teams. Do not omit the spelling quiz.

Page 22

Only the vowel *e* at the end of a word is able to make another vowel in the word say its name such as *base* and *home*. An *e* between two consonants itself says its short sound as in the word *never*.

Note that the exceptions for some words that end with a suffix or for compound words, such as *baseball* and *homework*, will be addressed later.

If there are two or more consonant blockers between a vowel and the end *e*, then the end *e* no longer has the ability to make a vowel to say its name.

After you have the student read *a-e (ape)*, *i-e (time)*, etc., write *appe* and *timme* on the board.

- Ask students to read what you have just written.
- Remind students that now the e cannot send its courage past two blockers, so the e is still silent and the vowels can only say their *short* sound.
- They should read these words as *ap* and *tim.*

The information at the bottom of the page explains that when an *e* is at the end of a word and it is the only vowel in the word, it says its name as in words *be* and *we*.

Page 23

More practice with <u>e</u> at the end of words. Give spelling quiz, praise 100%, and analyze any errors. If you are teaching more than one student, give praise to students who volunteer their mistakes and thank them for giving other students the opportunity to learn as well. We all benefit when we can help each other and also learn from each others' mistakes.

Page 24

This is a fun page for most students. It shows how the adding of an end *e* changes the pronunciation of the vowel in the word as well as its meaning.

Page 25

This page allows students to put into practice all that they have learned thus far:

- · Short vowels
- · Long vowel teams
- · Words ending in *e*
- · Words with *ew*

After reading the lists, but *before* giving the quiz, discuss any words that you or the students may think might cause spelling problems. You may break the quiz into four sections, giving 2-3 words for each column.

Review rules. Also, remind students to spell from left to right while writing the sounds as they hear them.

Remind students to use the correct vowel teams, for example, to note the word requires *ay, ae, ai* or *a-e*. Also, note *ue* and *ew* words.

Page 26

Students will practice reading large words they have never seen before. These silly, made-up words are intended to provide decodable text for all students. These words serve to "level the playing field," for those who have some phonemic awareness as well as for those who are just learning, with an equal opportunity to decode and apply phonemic decoding strategies to words that none of the students have ever seen.

Additionally, some students may have been taught to substitute familiar words when they encounter unfamiliar ones. When students do this, however, this means that they cannot grow beyond what they already know.

This activity will prepare them for reading words outside their knowledge base. It is essential for students to grow beyond their familiar knowledge base.

This page also teaches students to not be afraid of big words. In addition, it provides practice using context clues. Context clues are used for deciphering the *meaning of a word*, not necessarily to "figure out" how to guess at pronouncing a word.

This page further introduces students to the use of context clues to build their understanding of the meanings of new words, that is, build vocabulary.

Sometimes context is used to determine pronunciation based on one's aural vocabulary.

A NOTE ABOUT HETERONYMS:

Hetero [different] *nyms* [names] are words that have the same spelling as another, but a different sound, that is "names," and meaning.

Example: *He was sent to the first **row** in the classroom after he got into a **row** with the boys in the back.*

Example: *Please read the book to me after you have read it to your sister.*

Explanation: Regional dialects indicate pronunciation variations that may have arisen because of natural or human-made barriers.

A NOTE ABOUT ACCENTS AND DIALECTS:

In some regions, the word for attorney is pronounced *loyer* but in other regions the word is pronounced according to standard phonics rules, *lawyer*.

Some people pronounce the state name of Missouri according to standard phonics rules, while others may pronounce it as *Missouruh*.

Pronunciations may be affected by dialects; spellings generally remain constant.

Emphasize the last four points on page 26.

BEFORE YOU BEGIN THE SPELLING QUIZ:

You may choose one or both of the two silly long words on this page to give as a spelling quiz.

Have students notice where the vowel teams of ai, ay, and ae appear in each word.

Remind students that learning takes effort and attention.

Therefore, they need to pay attention to these same-sounding vowel teams in the words. When students read and study, they should pay attention to (a) how sounds are spelled and (b) where they appear in the word.

For example, praytzanmaizepple is pronounced the same as praitzanmayzepple. The first spelling is not the "correct" spelling of the word as written on p. 26.

Prior to the spelling quiz, discuss letters or combinations that might cause trouble.
As you dictate the words, enunciate the phonemes slowly and clearly, two or three times, if necessary.

Remember that accurate spelling requires practice but will improve over time when the student follows decoding/encoding rules is alert and has analytical focus as he or she reads.

Remind the students to say the sounds as they write what they hear.
Follow correction procedure.

Page 27

Y at the end of a word with another vowel in it says "eeee".

When there is an e at the end of a word with another vowel in it, the e is silent; it does not say its vowel name.

After completion of this page, students should no longer confuse and misspell words like *babe* for baby or *sore* for sorry in their reading and writing.

Page 28

When *y* is by itself in a word and at the end of a word, it says *i* as in *kite*.

Depending on the age of the students, you may want to have them form their arms and body into a Y, and then use their pointer fingers to point at themselves. When they do the latter, they should say "I."

Page 29

When students come across a *y* in a word it may cause confusion. Sometimes it has the short i (igloo) sound as in the word *myth*. The *y* also may sounds like the long *i(kite)* as in the word *typhoon*.

Spelling tricks are helpful for students to remember correct spelling. A few examples are given on this page. Sometimes, however, it just takes time, effort, and experience to learn the correct spelling and pronunciation. Remind students that it is much easier to memorize one letter in a word than it is to remember the entire word.

For example, the word, *gymnastic,* has nine letters and follows phonetic rules. The students merely need to remember that the *y* in this word is pronounced with a short *i (igloo)* sound.

The rules that *gymnastic* follows are:
- Words with *gy* make the *g* have the *j* sound (pages 67-68).
- The vowel by itself says its sound (a, apple and i, igloo, page 1).
- When *c* is at the end of the word, it has a *k* sound (page 62).

The rest of the consonants are pronounced in standard fashion.

In the word *typist*, the *y* has a long *i* sound. Again, the word follows the rules. Therefore, students merely need to remember that this word is spelled with a *y* and it has the long *i* (kite) sound.

This page also presents the *psy-* troublemaker. It gives its origin, thus explains why students may have difficulty with this combination. Students enjoy information about word origins. This page also gives a quick reference for vocabulary development in the teaching of the ending *-ology*.

Remember to give the spelling quiz. Do not forget to ask how many got 100%, one wrong, or two wrong. Compliment successes and improvements.

Ask for volunteers to share any misspelling of the words. Write the words as misspelled. Discuss and analyze their errors so that other students will develop the habit of using these strategies to correct their own spellings.

If necessary, you may want to separate and write the syllables from top to bottom, as follows:

gym

nas

tic

Help students to understand that they can read small words and word parts across from left to right. Therefore, they can read large words across, reading from left to right, one sound at a time as g-y-m-n-a-s-t-i-c.

Page 30

This page helps students understand why some words break the rules. It explains that other English-speaking countries pronounce *our* troublemakers just as they are spelled. We say that *they* have an accent when *they* speak.

On the other hand, they may say that *we* have an accent when we speak. It is fun for students to read both dialect variations with both the short and long vowel sounds.

Give the spelling quiz for these words at the end of page 31.

Page 31

Stress correct spelling and make sure to review the three numbered spelling strategies. Do this activity quickly and follow it with a spelling quiz.

Remember to give the spelling quiz. Do not forget to ask how many got 100%, one wrong, or two wrong. Compliment successes and improvements. Ask for volunteers to share any misspelling of the words. Write the word on the overhead as it was misspelled. Discuss and analyze their errors so that other students will develop the habit of using these strategies to correct their own spellings.

Page 32

This page presents some explanation as to why English seems so confusing. Remember the better you are able to explain why English is spoken and written the way it is, the less confusing it will become for most of your students.

Have the students pronounce the Old English word #3. It would seem that over the years, people began what they heard, and wrote accordingly.
Note word #11, *what,* at times, was spelled *hwaet.*

Although we usually tell students that the *wh* = the "breath sound," the letters *w* and *h* together confuse some students who want to read "wuh huh." Explain to students that the reason the *wh* = the breath sound is that, at one time, the wh in many words was once written *hw.*

This is an excellent example of how words have been changed in spelling and pronunciation over the years.

Page 33

Two spelling methods are given to assist students to tackle words that are troublemakers. Go over both ways to allow students to familiarize themselves with these strategies.

> Remind students to be attentive readers and pay attention to how words are spelled.!

Page 34

Students can use many "tricks" to help them spell correctly. Have students learn these tricks and to be alert for words that have tricks like these, such as saying *Wed-nes-day* when they are spelling *Wednesday.*

Page 35

Reading from left to right is such an important skill that the program has devoted a full page to reinforcing this skill. Studies found that fastest and most accurate readers do not look at the whole word. Instead, their eyes move rapidly across the words reading from left to right, quickly noticing each letter. Many students will have to retrain themselves. This will probably be difficult.

Automaticity and increased fluency will come with time and practice.

A hint is to have them place their finger or pencil at the <u>beginning</u> of each word, moving across the word left to right under each sound as it is pronounced.

Avoid placing their finger, etc. at the *middle* of a word. If they do so, it may cause them to focus on the whole word configuration and distract them from reading from left to right.

Although this may seem tedious, the good news is that the more students practice this skill, the more quickly they will become fluent and accurate readers as well as better spellers.

MAKE SURE STUDENTS READ THE WORD ALL THE WAY THROUGH.
THE **LAST LETTER** IS JUST AS IMPORTANT AS THE **FIRST**.

When analyzing spelling errors have students read the word as it is spelled with the errors.
For example:

- If the student spelled the word *sorry* as *sore*, have the student read the word as he/she wrote it using the phonics rules to pronounce the word.
- Ask the student how *sorry* should be written to have *e*'s name or the long *e* sound at the end of the word. (Remind the student, if necessary, of the rule on page 27.)

Reading a word (according to the phonics rules) as they wrote it, teaches students to self-correct. They may be able to know that a word does not "look right." Moreover, they will know what to do to spell it correctly.

Give students the opportunity to correct their own mistakes.

Ask what the students need to do to correctly spell any errors.

When students mispronounce words, the teacher can use this as a "teachable moment." When correcting students you can do the following:

- Slowly read the word from left to right enunciating the sounds clearly, so they can hear and notice the difference.
- Have the student identify the error and then correctly read the word from left to right.

Page 36

The aw is a big troublemaker (as notated by the green lettering and ™). Students often confuse *aw* for *ow*. For example, they may miss-read the word *brown* for the word *brawn*.

When teaching this *aw* sound, oval mouth shape is most important for correct pronunciation. [One teacher had her students pretend to put a whole egg in their mouths and then pronounce the words.]

Always be mindful of building vocabulary. You might ask, "Are there any words whose meanings you do not know?" Again, you quickly may give the definition and a sentence, but move on. You may go back later and do further vocabulary development.

On the other hand, depending on your time, you may want to take a few minutes to have the student write the definition and sentence for one or two words or use new words throughout the day.

You want to get through this program quickly because older students need to be familiar with phonics strategies so that they can be used throughout in other daily reading requirements in other classes, etc.   With ability to use decoding strategies, students will be able to read most words in the English language, estimated to be around 1,000,000.

IMPORTANT!   When teaching this to a large group, make sure to include the more skilled readers who may get bored. You may want to involve these readers by having them read some of the text. This prevents their boredom. Moreover, they may learn something they did not know before.

PHONICS ISN'T ONLY FOR STRUGGLING READERS

One "gifted" student who was in a class thought she was a good reader. In fact, she was the best reader among very poor readers. However, she went through this program at the beginning of the year with the rest of the class and used its strategies throughout the school year.

Her end-of-the-year standardized tests showed that she had gone from reading merely *on level* upon entering 6th grade in August to reading at a post high school level by May.

Page 37

The *au* is also a troublemaker and it has the same sound as *aw*. Have the entire class read the word lists stressing the *au* sound. You may continue with the second half of the page or give a short spelling quiz of the *au* words only.

The middle section of this page briefly addresses accent marks, a dictionary skill. This may be new for some students and a review for others. Read or relate this information to the students.

The ia and iu endings in words both have the long e (tree) sound then the short u (up) sound. After reading these words aloud, give a spelling quiz. Follow the spelling quiz procedure as explained previously for page 36.

Page 38

Practice the *aw* words and *au* words together. Select volunteers or randomly select students to read the sentences aloud.

Give a dictation quiz using one or two of the sentences.
- Enunciate slowly and very clearly. Give students time to process.
- Repeat dictated sentences once or twice.
- Remind students to read the sentences back to themselves.
- Have them proofread what they actually wrote, not what they think they wrote.
- Follow spelling quiz procedure.

Page 39

The short and long *oo* page may go quickly. Differences in pronunciation possibly came from different groups using similar sounds. Both long and short *oo* sounds are made with similar lip/mouth formation. Eventually when words were written down, these sounds came to be written the same.

Be sure to discuss the words should, would, and could. In the program, the l's in these words are printed in white, which means they are written but not spoken.

Again, note that local, regional dialect will influence the pronunciation of these and other words.

Page 40

Students like this page. It is straightforward and simple. This is often referred to as "r-controlled" vowels. That is because short a (apple) plus /r/ are not pronounced as /ăr/, rather /ŏ/ as in ox + r.

The *ar* in words will always have the "controlled a sound" as in the word car. Tell the students when they hear "r" in a word, they must write *ar.*

Read these words together as a class at a fast pace.

- Discuss any words that may cause a problem in spelling, for example, _March_ and _march_. Remind students of words can sound alike but have different meanings.
- Give quick definitions and sentence examples.
- Students may use dictionaries to look up one or two words.

Do not belabor this activity. **Keeps the lesson moving at a brisk pace.**

You may want to have other vocabulary-development activities at another time or assign for homework.

Also, bring attention to any words that may cause a problem in spelling.

Remember to give the spelling quiz and follow spelling correction procedure. Although the words on this page will be easy for most students to spell, do not break from procedure.

Read the lists, follow vocabulary development and quiz procedures, and move on.

Page 41

This page is self-explanatory and easy. *Or* always says ōr. Read the lists, follow vocabulary development and quiz procedures and move on.

Page 42

"R-controlled" words with no silent shadow e at the end will all be pronounced the same: *er, ir, ur.* Words with er, ir, and ur will be *easier to read than to spell* because students have to remember when to use the correct combination in spelling. The pronunciation is the same for these combinations. Give a spelling quiz at the end of each column so that students will not be confused. It will take more time, practice, and study for students to learn which of these combinations is required for these words.

Pages 43- 49

INTRODUCTION TO DIGRAPHS

These are important and difficult for English language learners because they are two consonants that create one unique sound.

Throughout these pages, a bit of history is given on how these digraphs came about. The *Phonics Steps to Reading Success* program calls these the *H Combos* because they all use the *h* to create the single phoneme.

Teach that a digraph (di=two / graph=write) means that two letters are written for one sound.

For vocabulary development, depending on time constraints, you can give the meaning of any unknown words, or model dictionary skills to look up the meaning. Also, you may assign this task to a student(s) who already understands this concept.

Page 43

The first digraph is *ch* as in the words *choo-choo, chip*. English language learners may need more help with digraphs. As with any part of the program, make sure to correct students who are pronouncing sounds incorrectly. If teachers do not correct students in an attempt to avoid embarrassing them, it may cause students problems in the future. Teach effectively and correct as necessary. Be kind, patient, positive, and consistent. Always, help students to excel to their highest potential.

For students having difficulty, practice the *ch* sound with the class by having the students say the words *choo-choo, chip*. You may also have them pretend to sneeze and say, "Ah-choo!" Keeping that sound in mind, they can say the word. Repeat as necessary.

About English learners: Note that some mouth muscles required to speak English may have been flexible when the student was an infant but may have fallen into disuse if the native language is a non-English language. Those unused muscles in the mouth area must be strengthened with practice as is done with any weakened muscle. Generally, with practice, concentration, and effort, pronunciation will improve. Fluency will follow.

Model the *ch* digraph yourself by strongly emphasizing the pronunciation of the ch digraph. The *ch* digraph has a strong, bold sound. Many English language learners who do not have this sound in their language frequently pronounce *ch* as a soft /sh/ sound. They may say *ship* instead of *chip* or *shop* instead of *chop*. It is imperative to correct this error in a respectful manner.

In a Classroom Setting

Students who are having problems will hear the correct pronunciation without being singled out all of the time. Of course, you can focus on a correction.

- For example, if the class is reading the lists as a group and you hear someone say *snack* instead of *sack*, stop. Do not continue.
- You may say, "Let's try that again. Read each sound left to right."
- Do not spend much time on a difficult word.
- Discuss any problem-causing aspects, then review and have class read the word left to right, then move on.

IMPORTANT!

In a group or class, do not spend too much time on just one or two, but it is imperative that all students are taught correctly.

- If individuals need more practice, schedule time to go over this with them after school or at lunchtime.
- Under certain circumstances, you may students them with others such as a volunteer or teaching assistant, who can model correct pronunciation. Make sure the volunteer or teaching assistant is trained, supportive and encouraging.
- While using capable students in the classroom as helpers sometimes is acceptable, generally, do not rely on these students to be responsible for working with the less capable students during class time.
- Do not use stronger students as unpaid tutors.
- More capable students must be permitted to advance their *own* academic accomplishments during class time, fulltime.
- Older, trained, students or capable classmates may want to help in an after-school volunteer program.

☞ **CORRECTION IS ESSENTIAL!** Correct with humor and respect, but always correct.
If **you** don't correct, students may never learn.

- To some observers, it may seem harsh to correct a student's pronunciation particularly in the upper grades. Nevertheless, it is a major disservice to the student when errors are not addressed and corrected.
- All correction must be given in a positive manner, never rudely or mockingly.
- Explain to all students that you are preparing them for their future and that school is a safe place to learn. Your classroom should be a safe place for learning. Never allow any student to laugh at another's mistakes.
- Reinforce successes. It is up to the teacher to set the standard for respect and support of all students. Explain that the classroom is the place to make mistakes. It is better to learn from mistakes in the classroom than to be embarrassed elsewhere.
- Be direct. Explain to students that in the world outside of school, people may not openly comment on people's mispronunciations in a job interview, in conversation, or other situations, but people *will* notice. Again, the classroom is the place to learn.

To enunciate means to pronounce clearly. Stress the need for enunciation. This will not only help students to read and speak clearly, it will also help with spelling accuracy.

For example, the word *chimney* is often mispronounced as *c h i m **i** n e y*. As a result, it is often spelled incorrectly. Model the correct pronunciation *chim • ney.* Explain to students how the incorrect pronunciation can also lead to misspelling.

After students have read the lists of words, ask them to point out words that might cause spelling problems for them or others.

If you ask students to look for words that might cause other students problems, they will often point out words that are problematic for them. Follow spelling quiz procedures.

Page 44

This page offers a significant help in spelling as well as reading.

The "t-blocker" must be present between a short vowel sound followed by *ch* digraph as in catch.

The "t-blocker" is pronounced but ever so slightly. It is as if the strong crisp sound of *ch* camouflages the *t*.

If the word has a vowel team, there is no need for the blocker.

If there is another consonant acting as the blocker, as in the word ranch, there is no need for the "t-blocker."

There are always exceptions, as in the word "rich and which."

You have already emphasized to students that they are to spell words by writing their sounds from left to right in the order that they are heard. Because the *t* is seemingly silent in the *-tch* words, make sure that the students are keenly aware of the "t-blocker" rule.

The following are common spelling errors when this principle is *not* applied:

cach   swich   skech

The correct spellings are: *ca_tch   swi_tch   ske_tch*

If students are having difficulty, you may want to have them put an arrow <u>under</u> the short vowel pointing up to the vowel and put an arrow <u>over</u> the blocker pointing down to the blocker.

↓   ↓

Example: **d i t ch   r a n c h**

↑   ↑

Have student(s) explain this strategy to make sure they understand the concept.

Teach the difference in enunciation, spelling, and meaning of the words *pitcher* and *picture*. This is a common mistake, but can be avoided easily by following the basic phonics principles. After students read the lists of words, discuss which words need special attention for correct spelling. Follow spelling quiz procedures.

Page 45

After students read the lists of words, discuss which words need special attention for correct spelling. Follow spelling quiz procedures.

Page 46

The *sh* digraph is a softer sound and should not be confused with the ch digraph.

Students enjoy the etymology of words. More history is given this time regarding the development of the s͟h digraph. You might share with students that a skipper is in charge of a ship. Was a skipper once a "shipper?" Depending on your student(s), you may discuss how this variation might have come about.

After students read the lists of words, discuss which words need special attention for correct spelling. Follow spelling quiz procedures.

Frequently remind students: "Always find out why you made errors - if you have made any. Learn from your mistakes. Then, you won't make them again."

Page 47

A brief history is given on the development of the *th* digraph. Practice the pronunciation of this digraph following the directives in the center box. Again, this is a difficult digraph for English language learners.

After students read the lists of words, discuss which words need special attention for correct spelling. Follow spelling quiz procedures.

Page 48

The *ph* is a digraph that is a troublemaker. Teach this sound as /f/.

Explain this page discussing which letters or vowels may cause trouble in pronunciation and or spelling. Many visual clues are given on this page to help with decoding.

After students read the lists of words, again discuss which words need special attention for correct spelling. Follow spelling quiz procedures.

Page 49

This page explains how to produce the sound of the *wh* digraph. As noted on information at page 32, many *wh*-words of today were originally spelled and pronounced *hw*. Often, when the words eventually were "codified" into written language as in the dictionary, the commonly accepted spelling became *wh* but the *hw* sound remained with us. These spellings today cause troubles for unsuspecting learners!

This page is rich in words for vocabulary development. After students read the lists of words, again discuss which words need special attention for correct spelling. Follow spelling quiz procedures.

FYI : A BIT MORE OF THE HISTORY OF ENGLISH

The Great Vowel Shift was a major change in the <u>pronunciation</u> of the <u>English language</u>, occurring between the 14th and 15th centuries. The shift continued for some time into the <u>16th century</u>, spreading outward from the metropolitan and port areas.

It represented a change in the long <u>vowels</u> (*i.e.,* a <u>vowel shift</u>). Vowel pronunciation has continued to change to this day, although it is much, much slower.

The long vowels form the main difference between the pronunciation of <u>Middle English</u> and <u>Modern English</u>, and the Great Vowel Shift is one of the historical events marking the separation of Middle and Modern English. Originally, these vowels had values much like those remaining in liturgical <u>Latin</u>.

However, during the Great Vowel Shift, two forms of long vowels became <u>diphthongs</u>, and the other five underwent an increase in tongue height and one of them came to the front. Simply put, to pronounce the long vowels of Middle English, one had to shift the pronunciation upwards in the mouth, meaning that a vowel that used to be pronounced in one place in the mouth would be pronounced higher up in the mouth in Modern English, as the *ee* sound in *meet* and the *u* sound in *fool*.

More advanced information can be found on Internet.   Search word examples: linguistics, mouth, vowels, *Great Vowel Shift,* Old English audio.

Minimally, you should take note of the changes regarding vowels as well as consonants; however, the more that you know regarding linguistics, the more you will be able to enrich your students' knowledge and the better educator you will be.

Page 50

It may take some time for students to learn these troublemaker (™) teams.

Explain to the students that at one time, the pronunciation of words like these were somewhat different. For example, all letters' sounds may have been pronounced. You may try to let the students read /s/ /ī/ /g/ /n/, with a guttural g. Over the years we have dropped the guttural pronunciations, but the old spelling vestiges remain.

Although this page may take a bit longer, depending on students English skills, read each team three times, as in / ī i l d / / ī i l d / / ī i l d / and, if necessary, read the lists two or three times. Discuss meanings, but, again, do not belabor lessons.

As mentioned earlier, as circumstances dictate, once you have completed the program, you may want to return to this page as a review or if you notice students are having difficulties when encountering these troublemakers.

Give as much spelling practice and review as needed for these troublemaker teams. Follow spelling quiz procedure

FYI: A LITTLE BIT MORE OF THE HISTORY OF ENGLISH

Depending on the level of your students, you might consider briefly explaining a bit more of the occurrence of the Great Vowel Shift in the English language.

Briefly clarify for your student(s) that English is a "fluid" language, with the influence of many other languages mixing like many streams flowing into one river. Each (language) "stream" brought with it its own pronunciations and spellings.

During the development of the English language in the Middle Ages, most people could not read and/or write. As more people began to learn how to read and write, many just guessed at spellings. There were no dictionaries or unified spelling rules.

When scholars finally agreed on standard spelling, many of these words kept their original spelling although the pronunciation had evolved. On the other hand, many words kept their original pronunciation but the spelling evolved.

As a result, many words have come down to us through history the way they were spelled and/or pronounced more than 500 years ago during the Middle Ages. Readers and writers in the 21st century are faced with history's mish-mashed legacy of words. The *Great Vowel Shift* has not ended.

The *i* in words ending in *-ild* and *-ind* is pronounced as the *i* in the word *time*.

It is hard to imagine that people once pronounced the *g* in words like *sign* or pronounced the *gh* in words like *flight*. In our speech today, the *gh* is not pronounced. Unfortunately, the silent *g* and *gh* stayed around to cause spelling problems for children and adults alike.

Also, if you are interested in hearing how Old English sounds, you may find further information on the Internet. If you have Internet capability, just type in search words such as, *Old English audio*.

Page 51

Students will now apply all the reading strategies that they have learned thus far.

On this page, there are twelve made-up words. The use of made-up words was done for various reasons. Primarily, all students will have an equal opportunity to apply what they have learned. Often, there are students in a class who know phonics techniques or who have an extensive vocabulary base. Therefore, these students have an ease of reading words that are familiar to them.

However, students who do not have such a base and are learning to use phonics strategies can be intimidated. With unfamiliar words, all students must apply learned phonics skills to decode unfamiliar or "invented" words that are new to all students in the class. In other words, "The playing field is leveled."

Moreover, throughout one's life experiences, we all encounter words that are unfamiliar when reading for education, pleasure, legal documents, etc. The professional jargon of doctors, lawyers, computer specialists or any other specialized field is filled with often large and challenging words.

Some entrepreneurs who know the benefits and effectiveness of explicit phonics are offering services to professionals, such as physicians and pharmacists, for whom non-phonics reading strategies such as substitution or getting the gist are not sufficient.

Furthermore, the fullest appreciation of literature written by such influential authors as James Joyce, Shakespeare, and J.R.R. Tolkien can be had by only those who are not intimidated by large unfamiliar words.

In preparation for the reading of the words and for the spelling quiz, direct students to take note of the various vowel teams: for example, *ay* and *ai* have the same long "a" sound. The second letter of these vowel teams is silent. Also, they should note what the silent vowel team member is and where it is in the word.

Particularly note word # 4 with its _ay_ and _ai_ teams. Teach your students to become "active readers." This will help them to take note of **which vowel teams are used** and **where they appear in a word**. For example, in our invented words, they both appear in one word, _qu**ay**th**ay**p**ai**n._

Students will also want to note any other spelling exceptions (troublemakers) that may cause confusion. Follow spelling quiz procedures.

Page 52

After students read the sentences, give one or two of the sentences as spelling dictation. Speak clearly. Enunciate each word well. Allow time for processing and writing. Follow spelling quiz procedures.

Be certain that the students read all words in each sentence correctly. If the reader substitutes a word, always correct. For example, in sentence # 6, the reader may say, "The sight of a bright light might frighten…."

Caution: Often, when children are taught sight words or the use of "word families" or rhyming words, they will get into a pattern of rhyming. When this happens, remind them to read each letter's sound, left to right.

Page 53

More practice with _ue, ui_ vowel teams and the _ew_™ (troublemaker) team. Review this strategy again. After students read the lists of words, discuss which words need special attention for correct spelling.

As always, ask the students if there are any words of which they do not know the meaning. You may quickly tell them, giving an example, look it up in a dictionary, or, for the sake of keeping the lesson moving, you may put the word on a list to be looked up later. Follow spelling quiz procedures.

Page 54

The sound of _ew_ has already been addressed on the previous page; however, another vowel combination that has the same sound is _eu_. Therefore, _eu_ and _ew_ both sound like the _long u._

This is an excellent page for vocabulary development as well as a linguistics lesson for older students. Using an unabridged dictionary, you can demonstrate why "new" is pronounced as "noo" or by discovering the origins of this "new" word. "Out with the old; in with the new."

Remember to discuss any words that need special attention for correct spelling. Follow spelling quiz procedures.

Page 55

This page covers the pronunciation of names. It is very difficult to pronounce names because names are personal. People do not always follow phonetic rules when spelling or pronouncing their own names. Therefore, teach students to follow the phonetic rules; or, if the correct, preferred pronunciation is in question, teach them to ask politely for the pronunciation. No spelling quiz needed for this page.

Page 56

The _ow_ and _ou_ are troublemakers because they do not have one standard, consistent, accepted pronunciation. The influence of the Great Vowel Shift is seen in these words.

Tell students that the *ow* and *ou* are spellings and pronunciations that have been passed down to us through history.

The *ow* can be pronounced as "Ow" as in, "Ow! That hurts!"
The *ow* can also be pronounced as the *long o* as in the word *snow* as:

*The girl with the **bow** in her hair walked through the **snow**.*

The only way to know for sure which ow sound is needed for correct pronunciation is to rely on one's prior knowledge, through context clues, or to consult a dictionary.

The *-ous* comes from the French or Norman influence. When **-ous** is at the end of a word, it generally indicates that the word is an **adjective**, as in the word *momentous*. The *-ous* is pronounced as /us/.

Words with the **-us** ending are most often from a Latin **noun**. When *-us* is at the end of a word, it generally indicates that the word is a noun as in the word, *circus*.

General Spelling hint:
If the word ending is spelled with **–us**, it is pronounced /us/ and it is a **noun** as *circus*.
If the word ending is spelled with **–ous**, it is pronounced /us/ and it is an **adjective** as *famous*.

Until students become accomplished readers, the following are suggested guidelines:
When reading an unfamiliar word with ou or ow, use the most common pronunciation of ou, ow, that is, the "hurt sounds" as in "Ouch!" and "Ow!"

If it does not "make sense" in the sentence, then advise students to try the secondary pronunciations of *ow* as in snow, *ou* as in through, *ou* as in *rough* /ruf/. (This will be explained on page 58).

English learners, of course, will have to rely heavily on a dual-language dictionary.

After students read the lists of words, discuss which words need special attention for correct spelling. Follow spelling procedures.

Page 57
More practice reading *ow/ou* words.
Have students read the sentences. Then dictate a sentence for spelling practice. Acknowledge those with 100%. Discuss and analyze errors.

Page 58
The *gh* combination can be a conundrum for both students and adults alike. This page focuses on *gh* in the middle and at the end of words. Generally, this *gh* combination is silent. However, with some words ending with *gh*, it is pronounced as /f/.

Less common sounds for the *gh* ending are /p/ and /k/. These sounds of *gh* are not addressed in the program because they are rare or out of use. The word *hiccough* (high cough) is a troublemaker. Notice that the *gh* is pronounced /p/. The spelling of this word has morphed into *hiccup*.

The *gh* in the words *hough* and *lough* have the /k/ sound; however, these words, although they may be found in an unabridged dictionary, are no longer in common use today. Follow spelling procedures.

Page 59

This page introduces letter combinations that do not consistently follow the common short vowel rules. Conventional pronunciation of Standard English, as spoken in most regions of the United States, usually alters the short *a* pronunciation in some words when the letter *a* is followed by the letter *i*.

These words have come down to us through history. Most likely, the spellings are remnants from the time when the English language was being written before spellings and pronunciations had been established and codified. Thus, the **al** combinations have been preserved with different pronunciations.

The *al* in words with *alt, alk* and *all* combinations usually have the *aw/au* sound. Remember the teams of *alt, alk, all, aught,* and *ought* all have the same initial sound. They are pronounced as aw/au as in the words *paw* and *auto*.

The conventional short a (apple) sound takes precedence for some words and names such as *Allan, Alex, allergy*, and *alibi*.

As with any sound, if students are having difficulty producing the sound, make sure that they are shaping their mouths correctly. As mentioned earlier, you may want to have the students use a mirror, if necessary.

After students read the lists of words, discuss which words need special attention for correct spelling. Note the word, false, with its silent e. Follow spelling quiz procedures.

Page 60

Give your students a moment to think about this question. They may respond with the /k/ or /s/ sound, or they may not respond. Read the answer at the bottom and go to page 61.

Page 61

Many students do not realize that it is so easy to know when to pronounce the hard or soft sound of c. When the letter c is followed by an e, i, or y, the c has the sound of s. This rule is very consistent.

Page 62

If another letter (besides e, i, or y), follows the letter c, then the c makes the k sound. When c is the last letter in a word, it is always pronounced the same way as the letter k. Exception: the *ch* digraph.

Page 63

This is a practice page is for students to apply what they have just learned.

Page 64

Answer key for page 63.

Page 65

Many readers who have not been explicitly taught this rule stumble when they read a word with double c's. This page will help with correct pronunciation of words that contain double c's.

In words such as *accomplish*, both c's have the k sound because of the letters that follow each c.

However, both c's do not always make the same sound. For example, the word *accessible* has double c.

- Some people may pronounce the word *accessible* correctly, meaning *readily used or reached*.
- Some people who do not understand this simple practical rule may pronounce this word incorrectly as *assessable* meaning, able to be estimated regarding size, quality, or value.

The first c in the word *accessible* has the k sound because the c is not followed by an e, i or y. The second c has the s sound because it is followed by an e.

Tell the student(s) to follow the rule, and they will pronounce both types of words correctly.

You may have the students practice, practice, practice the following saying, "When you see a ce, ci, cy, the c says /s/."

Page 66

When presenting this page, only give a moment for students to answer before giving them the answer at the bottom.

Page 67

History enriches the understanding of phonics. Make sure you expose the student to the reasons why words are pronounced the way they are. This particular rule is not as reliable as the *ce, ci , cy rule*.

However, teach the rule and the exceptions. Have students note the similarity between the written C and G. Early scribes (manuscript copiers) in the Middle Ages sometimes unintentionally interchanged them. The results are reflected in many words we use today.

Remind students that when they are in doubt about pronunciation, they need to consult the dictionary. It may seem that some students have to consult the dictionary quite often. Be positive. Encourage these students because this can be tedious work, and the students will want to give up. Do not let them give up!

Page 68

Remind students that the words which have color-coded red vowels or green letters are meant to assist them in their learning. Take note of irregular pronunciations such as *fugitive*.

Some nouns that end in the letter g can be changed into adjectives by doubling the *g* and adding *gy*. In this case, you are just doubling the first *g* or adding an identical blocker that is the same as the final consonant of the base, or root, word.

For example, the word **bug**gy is not pronounced *bug-jy*. It does not have the letter *j* sound even though it ends with a *gy*. These types of words are *exceptions*.

Page 69

This is the same type of review as done with the letter *c*. Depending on your classroom arrangement, you may want your student to write the answers on a separate sheet of paper or give the answers orally to you as you mark them.

Note words # 42 (longitude) and # 43 (legislate). You may find that your students pronounce the words long and leg and do not follow the gi /j/ rule. This may be because your students have been taught to look for little words in big words to help them pronounce correctly. You can see that this is not an effective strategy. If they do say longitude and legislate, then ask them to tell you what –gi- says. Then, tell them to try again by following the –gi (/ j /) rule.

Page 70

Answers for page 69.

Page 71

This page may be difficult for some students, especially English learners, because the short vowel sounds are slid into the -ng throat sound. For some students, you might have them put two fingers at their throat and say -ing, -ang, -ung. Have them exaggerate the hard g sound at the end. Make sure that you enunciate very clearly when modeling these words.

Again, explaining the historical aspect of how these sounds came to be will give students a broader knowledge base as to the development of the English language. Follow spelling procedures.

Page 72

The words on this page contain a s or z that in Modern English have evolved to sound like /zsh/. In this list of words, there are many *troublemakers*. Have the student(s) take note and discuss any if necessary.

Follow spelling procedures. Remember that spelling takes more effort. However, do not focus on the spelling right now. Move forward with the reading and you can return for more spelling drill as necessary.

Page 73

For many students, this page increases students' reading and spelling ability because it is such a foreign concept to them. Remind them with emphasis that when they see a *ti, ci,* or *si,* followed by a vowel then the *ti, ci,* or *si,* is pronounced /sh/.

The vowels after the *ti, ci,* and *si* keep their sounds. When the vowel a or o is the letter before the *ti, ci,* and *si,* the vowel will say its name.

Encourage students not to be intimidated by the large words on this page. Remind them to follow the rules, identify troublemakers, and read from left to right. Follow spelling procedures.

Page 74

This page is for more practice reading and spelling words containing *ti* in them. Follow spelling procedures.

Page 75

This page is for more practice reading and spelling words containing *ti* and *ci* in them. Follow spelling procedures.

Page 76

The program addresses syllabication because it can be a helpful tool in pronouncing words. However, this dictionary skill can be developed at another time.

Depending on your student's abilities, either skip this page or do a cursory presentation and plan to return to syllabication at another time, perhaps a more detailed format as circumstances require.

Page 77

This page is for more practice reading and spelling words containing *ti, ci,* and *si* in them. Follow spelling procedures. Feel free to give only ti- words first, then ci- and so on. Remind the students that as they read, they should take note of the spellings of words.

Page 78

The *oy* and the *oi* are not standard vowel teams. These two combinations are called diphthongs, and they have their own unique sound. Follow spelling procedures.

Page 79

This page is a review page. Follow spelling procedures.

Page 80

This information is valuable to students, especially English learners and students who have been taught to read using *word families*, such as b**ed**, r**ed**, l**ed** and say "fish**ed**" and "dress**ed**." Without their knowing there is a "rule" or concept to learn for these types of words, readers often make errors in their pronunciation and spelling.

However, once the *-ted/-ded* rule is mastered, these *-ed* past tense verbs usually are no problem.

For students who need extra help, tell them to <u>underline</u> the <u>-ed</u> and look for the letter that comes before it. You may also have them underline all *–ted* or *-ded* endings. If they have a *-ted/-ded*, the pronunciation is easy from there.

Page 81

Practice for *-ted/-ded* and *-ed* words.

Page 82

This page provides practice in the spelling of words that end in *-ed*. The purpose of this page is to provide spelling practice in changing a word from a present to past tense of *-ed* words.

If students are having difficulty finding the answers, depending on your time-constraints, limit their choices by suggesting two or three possibilities, including, of course, the correct one.

Page 83

This is a difficult page for some students who may be intimidated by the **qu** combination.

Page 84

This page contains much information. You will want to read all of it to add to your own knowledge base and understanding of basic etymology of our language through the influence of other languages and cultures throughout history.

As appropriate to your student's needs, you may read or relate all or portions of this information.

Page 85

Read the bullet points in the first column to students.

The prefixes and definitions in the second column can be used for quick reference and review. It is not necessary to teach these at this point because each will be independently taught on subsequent pages.

Page 86

Refer to teacher notes, ⊤. You may want to use an unabridged dictionary for a more in-depth analysis of and enhancement of your students' as well as your own *vocabulary* development.

While you are presenting the material to your students, be prepared to explain the word origins that may help to explain definitions and spellings as well as pronunciation of words in some cases.

Procedure:

·   Introduce the prefix.
·   Discuss the meaning.
·   Ask students to read the word list.
·   Discuss word meanings as influenced by the prefix.

Remember to give the spelling quiz. Do not forget to ask how many got 100%, one wrong or two wrong. Compliment successes and improvements. Ask volunteers to share any misspelling of the words. Write the word on the board or paper as it was misspelled. Discuss and analyze their errors so that other students will develop the habit of using these strategies to correct their own spellings.

The focus of this and subsequent prefix lessons is on the prefix and definition of the prefix presented. As appropriate for your student, you may want to use these words for another activity at another time. Assignments that you might consider may be as follows:

−   Have students look up the meaning of several or all of the words and write them in a sentence.
−   Once students know the definition of the prefix, you may have them deduce the meanings of the words in the list based on their knowledge of (a) the prefix, and (b) the base or root word. This may be an oral or written activity.
−   Not all words are clearly defined easily as prefix meaning + root word, such as abnormal, meaning "different from the normal." As we know, words and meanings evolve.
−   The students will then use a dictionary to compare the accuracy of their definition to that of the dictionary.
−   Have the student create a story using several of the words in the list.
−   Encourage students to use the words in their daily speech and written work.

Page 87

Follow the format above.

Page 88

For the top section, follow the format above.
Directions for the second half of page 88.

FIRST PASSAGE

Pre-reading activity:

·   Discuss the meanings of the words with prefixes in the first passage and provide background knowledge as necessary.
·   Prepare students with the following tips on "active reading" to aid comprehension.
  −   As the sentence is being read, concentrate on what is being read.
  −   As the sentence is being read, create a mental picture that the sentence depicts.

Reading:
– The teacher (or volunteer who is a fluent reader) should then read the first passage aloud, slowly and clearly.
– All students must follow along, reading the passage silently.
– If necessary, re-reading may be done either chorally or by one or more students,

Post-reading activity:
– Discuss the mental pictures created during the reading of the first sentence in the passage.
– Discuss meaning of passage.
– Do the same with the second sentence of the passage.
– The teacher should guide and make any corrections as needed.
– As appropriate, the teacher may want to use one or more of the sentences for spelling dictation practice.

SECOND PASSAGE

Follow the format for the first passage.

Pages 89
Follow the same format given for Page 86.

Page 90
Follow the same format given for Page 86.

For the sentences at the bottom of the page, follow the same format used for the first passage on Page 88.

Page 91
Follow the same format given for Page 86.

Page 92
Follow the same format given for Page 86.
For the sentences at the bottom of the page, follow the same format used for the first passage on Page 88.

Page 93, 94
Follow the same format given for Page 86.

Page 95
Follow the same format given for Page 86. For the sentences at the bottom of the page, follow the same format used for the first passage on Page 88.

Page 96
Follow the same format given for Page 86.
The information at the bottom of the page is for enrichment.

Page 97

Follow the same format given for Page 86.
For the sentences at the bottom of the page, follow the same format used for the first passage on Page 88.

Page 98 – 102

Follow the same format given for Page 86.

Page 103

Have students memorize, remember, and always spell the rule: "Write *i* before *e* except after *c*." This page presents information that will help students to accurately spell words that commonly cause problems for the average speller.

Remember to give the spelling quiz and follow the established procedures. You may also use the sentences for spelling dictation.

Page 104

Read the information for each of the bullet points.
Follow the established procedures for reading lists and spelling quiz.

~ ~

This is just the beginning.

Encourage the learner(s) to continue to read and to develop vocabulary by reading and using the dictionary and thesaurus. The more they read, the more they increase their vocabulary *and* their knowledge. Encourage them to read fiction and non-fiction in many areas, to grow beyond what they already know.

SOMETHING TO THINK ABOUT:

"Knowledge is power."   Sir Francis Bacon (1561 - 1626)

"Learning is not attained by chance; it must be sought for with ardor and attended to with diligence."   Abigail Adams (1744 - 1818)

"I count him braver who overcomes his own desires than him who conquers his enemies; for the hardest victory is the victory over self."   Aristotle (384-322 B.C.)

"Prepare yourself in all areas of life skills and knowledge. In the future, when you apply for a job and there are 500 other people applying for the same job, you want to be the best. Work now to succeed then."   S.M.David (unknown-1956)

"Whenever you are asked if you can do a job, tell 'em, 'Certainly I can!' Then get busy and find out how to do it."   Theodore Roosevelt (1858 - 1919)

"Leadership and learning are indispensable to each other."   John F. Kennedy (1917 – 1963)

BASIC RULES OF PHONICS
ALIGNED WITH PAT DORAN'S *PHONICS STEPS TO READING SUCCESS*

The following is included as a basic introduction to phonics principles taken from Pat Doran's Phonics Steps to Reading Success (PSRS). Presented compactly, the following basic rules are intended only as an overview or review and are not complete lessons.

Phonics is a Beginning Step to Reading
Readers must have the following skills:

- **Phonemic awareness:** *the ability to hear, identify, and manipulate sounds in words. Example: Say the word, **hat**, slowly and hear three sounds (phonemes) /h/ /a/ /t/. Say the word, **ship**, slowly and hear three sounds /sh/ /i/ /p/. Say the word, **fast**, slowly and hear four sounds as /f/ /a/ /s/ /t/.*

- **Phonics:** *the knowledge of the relationships between phonemes(sounds) and graphemes (letters that are used to represent the sounds.*

- **Vocabulary:** *the knowledge and ability to use information about meanings and pronunciations of words.*

- **Fluency:** *the ability to read text accurately and quickly.*

- **Comprehension:** *the ability to understand, remember, and communicate what was read from the written text.*

Page numbers refer to pages in *Phonics Steps to Reading Success*.

1. Read and spell from left to right. *(p. B-G)*
2. Be aware of the shape of your mouth as you pronounce sounds. *(p.1)*
3. When a vowel in a word stands alone, the vowel says its *short sound* and not its name, as in:

Vowel	Sound	Example
a	/a/	Ann's apple
e	/e/	Ed's egg
i	/i/	In the igloo
o	/o/	The ox says "Aaah." Open wide!
u	/u/	Up, up, umbrella

    (p.1)

4. Most words with a short vowel sound that end with the /k/ sound are spelled with *ck* at the end:
    tack   neck   pick   clock   duck *(p.4)*

[–ck Spelling tip]

(a)   Say the sounds as in the silly word, *smick*, left to right: /s/ /m/ /i/ /k/.
(b)   Say the sound /s/ as you write *s*.
(c)   Say the sound /m/ as you write m.
(d)   Then, say to yourself, "I hear a short i (igloo) sound and the /k/ sound."
(e)   Therefore, I must write *ick*.   *(p. 5)*

If a word contains any vowel <u>and</u> ends with the letter *e*, the final *e* is always silent.

(p. 8)

6.   If a word ends in *le*, pronounce the /l/ sound as in bundle; the *e* is silent and makes no sound.
(p. 8)

7. Vowels that appear together are called *vowel teams*. Generally, when two vowels are next to each other in a word, the first one says its *name* while the second one is *silent*. Thus, the old saying, "When two vowels go walking, the first one does the talking."   *(pp. 12-21)*

Vowel team	Examples
ae	m<u>ae</u>lstrom, G<u>ae</u>lic
ai	p<u>ai</u>l, m<u>ai</u>n, gr<u>ai</u>n
ay	p<u>ay</u>, st<u>ay</u>, M<u>ay</u>
ea	s<u>ea</u>m, l<u>ea</u>f, sp<u>ea</u>k
ee	m<u>ee</u>t, sl<u>ee</u>p, str<u>ee</u>t
ie	p<u>ie</u>, t<u>ie</u>d, sp<u>ie</u>d
oa	g<u>oa</u>t, t<u>oa</u>st, m<u>oa</u>n
oe	h<u>oe</u>, t<u>oe</u>, J<u>oe</u>
ue	bl<u>ue</u>, tr<u>ue</u>, contin<u>ue</u>
ui	s<u>ui</u>t, fr<u>ui</u>t, recr<u>ui</u>t *
ew	f<u>ew</u>, n<u>ew</u>, bl<u>ew</u> **

  * In the United States, ui is generally read with an /oo/ sound as in *moon*.
 ** ew is generally pronounced <u>e</u>u or *long u*; the letter *w* was once a *double u*.   *(pp. 10-21)*

8.   When a consonant is between a vowel and its silent, shadow teammate *e* – as in *ape* or *kite* – the consonant is called a *blocker*. In such a positioning, (a) the first *vowel* says its name, and (b) the *e* is silent.   *(p. 22)*
The following general rules apply:
•   The *e* is the only vowel whose influence can "pass through" the consonant blocker to make the vowel say its name.   *(p. 23)*

- The *e* can send its influence through only one consonant blocker, not two. In the word āpe the *a* says its name, but in *gaffe* or *appetite,* the *a* is pronounced as its short sound. Similarly, in kīte the *i* says its name, but in *ki<u>tt</u>en* the *i* says its short sound. *(pp. 22-25)*

9. A single *e* at the end of a word or syllable says its name:
    (a) when it is the single vowel in an entire word (*he, she, we, me*); and
    (b) when it is the last letter in a single-vowel syllable (*maybe*).   *(p. 22)*

10. When reading unfamiliar words, change the form of your mouth to pronounce each phoneme as it appears in the word.   *(p. 26)*

11. If a word with a vowel ends in *y*, then the *y* says /ee/ as in *fun<u>ny</u>*.
    Spelling tip: If you hear an /ee/ sound at the end of a word and there is another vowel in the word write *y* at the end. The word *s-o-r-e* does not say *sorry*.   *(p. 27)*

12. If a word with a vowel ends in *y*, the effect of *y* on the vowel is the same as that of a silent *e*. That is, the vowel is "forced" to say its name. Two blocker consonants between a vowel and final *y* keep the vowel short.
    Kitty is not *kity*.   *Bunny* is not *buny*.   *(p. 27)*

13. If *y* is the only vowel in a word, it is pronounced as long *i* as in *my, dry, cry*, and *fly*. *(p. 28)*

14. When *o* ends a word, the *o* it says its name as in *go, so, ego*, and *no*.   *(p. 28)*

15. When *y* is between consonants, it "acts like" the vowel *i*. It is either *long* or *short*. It is pronounced as short /i/ as in *myth, gypsy*, and *physical*. It is pronounced as *long i* in the words, *type, typist,* and *cypress.*
    Tip: Words with y often have regional variations. When in doubt, use a dictionary. *(p. 29)*

16. *Psych* is pronounced /sike/ as in *psychic, psychology*, and *psychiatry*.   *(p. 29)*

17. Some words break the rules, because the English language developed over several centuries. Other languages and a variety of dialects have influenced English and spelling.   *(p.30)*
    Tip: When in doubt of how to pronounce a word, first follow the rules. Then, if you are able, adapt the pronunciation of the word as it is commonly pronounced or use a dictionary. The "worst" that will happen is that you may pronounce the word with a slight variation from commonly accepted pronunciation or with a British, Scottish accent, and the like.
    Moreover, at least you will be able to make a reasonable attempt to pronounce the word that will neither impede fluency nor significantly digress from correct Standard English.   *(pp. 30-32)*

18. The sounds of *aw* and *au* are pronounced with the mouth shaped like an oval or an egg.
(pp. 36-38)

19. When *i* is followed by *a* or *u*, it is not a vowel team. The *i* is pronounced /ē/ as in *Maria, Austria, lithium.* (It seems easier to pronounce than ĭ/ă.) *(p. 37)*

20. The *oo* vowel digraph has either a long sound as in *moon,* or a short sound as in *foot.* When decoding, try using the long sound first. Generally, more words have the long sound than have the short sound. Other principles may apply. *(p. 39)*

21. The letter r affects the sound of the vowel that comes before it. Therefore, the vowel is called an r-controlled vowel.

ar	pronounced	/âr/	as in	*car, arm, bar, farm* *
or	pronounced	with a *long o* /or/	as in	*for, torn, born*
er	pronounced	/ûr/	as in	*verb, fern, herd*
ir	pronounced	/ûr/	as in	*girl, birth, fir*
ur	pronounced	/ûr/	as in	*fur, turn, spur*

   Spelling tip: When you are encoding sounds into symbols (spelling) and you hear what sounds like the *name* of the letter r, write "ar," as in *car.* However, when a *vowel team with a consonant blocker r (vc-e)* occurs, then the first vowel says its name and the final *e* is silent as in *fire, store, cure,* and *here.* *(pp. 40-42)*

22. The digraph *ch* is usually pronounced /ch/ as in *choo-choo* or *chip.* When *ch* follows a short vowel, a consonant blocker must be present as in *ditch, French,* and *match.* *(pp. 43-45)*

23. The digraph *sh* is pronounced /sh/ as in *ship, sheet, fish,* and *cash.* *(p. 46)*

24. The digraph *th* is pronounced /th/ by softly sticking the tongue behind the teeth and blowing out, as in *Thanksgiving, thick,* and *bath.* The digraph *th* can also be pronounced with a "harder" sound, by putting the tongue between the top and bottom teeth, blowing, and vibrating the tongue slightly as in *this, that,* and *those.* *(p. 47)*

25. The digraph *ph* is pronounced /f/ as in *phone, dolphin,* and *photo.* *(p. 48)*

26. The *digraph wh* can be pronounced /ʰw/ with a slight puff of air expelled as in *whale, when,* and *whim.* *(p. 49)*

27. The single vowel *i* is pronounced as *long i* as in the following exceptions:
   - *ild* words as *wild, mild, child;*
   - *ind* words as in *find, kind, blind;*
   - *ign* words as in *sign, design, resign** and
   - *igh* words as in *sigh, high, flight*.*

   *Note that in *-igh-* and *-ign- words,* the g is silent. *(p. 50)*

28.   The *eu* and *ew* teams are pronounced as long u, as in *dew, grew, deuce,* and *feud.* Say *long e* and *long u* <u>very</u> <u>quickly</u> together to say /eu/. You will hear *long u.*   *(p. 54)*

29.   The diphthongs *ow* and *ou* are pronounced as in "Ow! Ouch!" and words, such as *flower, wow, loud,* and *mouth.*
    - *Ow* can also stand for the *long o* sound as in *snow, show,* and *tow.*
    - The diphhthong *ou* can also stand for the /oo/ sound as in *through.*
    - The diphhthong *ou* is also pronounced as a *short u* when followed by the letter *s* as in *famous, momentous,* and *disastrous.*   *(p. 56)*

30.   The vowels in *alt, alk, aught, all, ought* have the *aw* sound as in *saw, walk,* and *taught.*   *(p. 59)*

31.   The letter *c* sounds like:
    - /s/ when followed by *e, i,* or *y* as in *center, citizen,* and *cymbal;*
    - /k/ when followed by *a, o,* or *u* as in *cash, coffee,* and *cup;* or
    - /k/ when it is the last letter of a word as in *picnic.*   *(pp. 60-65)*

32.   The letter *g* generally sounds like:
    - /j/ when followed by *e, i,* or *y* as in *gem, gin* and *gym* (with some exceptions such as *target, girl, gift);*
    - *hard g* when followed by *a, o,* or *u* as in *gash, go,* and *gush;* or
    - *hard g* when it is the last letter of a word as in *dog, dig* and *dug.*   *(pp. 66-70)*

33.   If a *ti, ci,* or *si* is followed by a vowel, it makes the /sh/ sound as in *option, cautious,* and *conscious.*   *(pp. 73-75)*

34.   Syllabication basics:
    (a)   *rab·bit, mur·mur,* and *mag·net.* The syllable is called *closed.*
    (b)   An "open syllable" often occurs when one consonant is between two vowels. The syllable is divided before the consonant as in *so·lo, spi·ral* and *ve·to.*
    (c)   A vowel may say its name when it is at the end of a syllable as in *fi-nance.*

          Tip: If this is a new word to the reader and the reader pronounces as *fin-ance* by following the short-vowel rules, he/she would be equally correct with perhaps a slight accent as may be heard in parts of England. See note at #18.

    (d)   With words ending in a consonant + le, the consonant + le pattern is considered to be a separate syllable, as in *han·dle, wrin·kle* or *pad·dle.*

    (e)   The following are usually separate syllables:
    - Vowel teams with blockers as in *con·crete* and *in·side;*
    - Vowel teams without blockers as in *de·feat, team·mate;* and
    - *R-controlled* teams as in hard·en, herd, fir, port·ly, and curt·ly.   *(p. 76)*

35. Diphthongs *oy* and *oi* are sounded by changing the mouth position first, to pronounce the sound of the first vowel (*long o*) and then, to slide quickly into the sound of the second vowel (*short i*). The result, *oi*, seems to make one unique phoneme as in *oil, point, toy,* and *joy*.

36. If *–ed* follows the letters *t* or *d*, it is pronounced *–ted* or *–ded*.
   - However, *-ed* is considered to be a separate syllable as in *plant·ed* and *raid·ed*.
   - If *–ed* follows any other letter, it is pronounced simply as /d/ or /t/ as in *harmed* (harmd) or *ripped* (ript) and the *–ed* is not a separate syllable.   *(pp. 80-82)*

37. The diphthong of *qu-* is usually pronounced /qw/ as in *queen, quit,* and *quest*. It is pronounced infrequently as /k/ in words with a French influence such as:
   - *-quet* as in *croquet;*.
   - *-quette* as in *croquette, etiquette,* and *briquette; and*
   - *-que* as in *antique, oblique,* and *catafalque*.   *(pp. 83-83A)*

38. Prefixes are syllables at the beginning of a word that modify or change the word.
   - Not all letter combinations that look like prefixes are actually prefixes.
   - One way to determine if a combination of letters *is* or *is not* a prefix is to remove the combination that resembles a prefix.
   - Sometimes (but not always), if a word remains, then the combination is a true prefix as in the words, *undone* and *supernatural*. However, if a word does not remain, it is not a true prefix as in *uncle*. When in doubt, use a dictionary.

   The most common prefixes and their meanings are:

ante-	before	pro-	before, for
anti-	against	re-	again, back
circum-	around	se-	aside
con-	with	sub-	under
de-	down, opposite, from	super- (*sur*)	above
dis-	apart, not, opposite	trans-	across
ex-	out	un-	not
in-	in	uni-	one
inter-	between, among	bi-	two
intra-, intro-	within	tri-	three
mis-	wrong		*(pp. 84-102)*

39. A troublemaking vowel team is *ie*. When this team is found in a word, it sometimes breaks the vowel-team rule. Namely, the <u>*i* is silent</u> and the <u>*e* says its name</u>, as in *piece, believe, achieve,*

In summary, explicit phonics teach that letter symbols represent corresponding sounds. For example, *a* represents the sound /a/ and the letter symbol *t* is the sound /t/. These letters written together represent the sounds /a/ /t/, that is, the word, *at*. After learning the phonemes represented by the consonant graphemes, reading (blending) the sounds from left to right across the word, students can read words such as the following:

/b/ /a/ /t/	bat	/c/ /a/ /t/	cat
/h/ /a/ /t/	hat	/m/ /a/ /t/	mat

With very few rules of phonics, students can also read words like *matador* and *catapult*. With the addition of the rule governing silent *e* and long vowels, students can easily decipher words like *entertainment, platitude,* and *gratitude*. Armed with phonics concepts, students gain the confidence to attack most words, even words that contain exceptions to the rules. When encountering an unfamiliar word, it is best for the reader to use phonics rules rather than skipping, substituting, or guessing. A dictionary is always a helpful tool to use when possible.

The Three Legs of Comprehension

Also note that successful reading comprehension is like a three-legged stool. If each leg isn't strong, firm, and even, the person sitting on the stool will always be balancing, wobbling, not "sitting successfully." The "legs" of the three-legged stool of successful comprehension are as follows:

1. Accurate decoding
2. Knowledge of the meanings of the words used in the passage(s) being read
3. Sufficient background knowledge to understand the passage(s) being read.

Phonics Steps to Reading Success focuses on accurate decoding and developing a larger vocabulary. With accurate decoding and increased vocabulary, readers will be able to read to expand their background knowledge with evermore information. Students will no longer be "wobbling" when they are reading.

Glossary of Selected Terms
Bibliography
Index

Glossary of Selected Terms

Adapted from Webster's New Twentieth Century Dictionary, Unabridged 2nd Edition.

Alphabet

Letters of a specific language in the order fixed by custom. Any system of letters or characters representing sounds.

The English Alphabet: *a b c d e f g h I j k l m n o p q r s t u v w x y z*

Consonant

Any speech sound produced by stopping and releasing the air stream (p,t,k,b,d,g), or stopping it at one point while it escapes at another (m, n, l, r), or forcing it through a loosely closed or very narrow passage (f, v, s, zh, sh, z, th, h, w, y), or by a combination of these means (ch, j).

Consonant Phonemes (see Phonemes)

/b/ bat   /c/ cat   /d/ dog   /f/ fish   /g/ gum   /h/ hat   /j/ jump   /k/ kite   /l/ lion   /m/ mop   /n/ nose   /p/ pig   /q/ (qu) queen   /r/ rat   /s/ sail   /t/ ten   /v/ van   / w web   /x/ ax   / z/ zigzag

Decode

Reading; to translate from a code (letter/symbol) into language (or sound)

Diacritical

Diacritical marks, sign, or point: any mark used with a letter or character to distinguish it from another to indicate how it is pronounced. Examples: ă, ū.

Diacritical marks, and so forth, are often explained at the bottom of dictionary pages.

Encode

Spelling; to convert sound into code (letter/symbol)

Phoneme

[Comes from the Greek, *phonema*, meaning a sound.] In linguistics, a class, or family, of closely related speech sounds regarded as a single and represented in phonetic transcription but the same symbol as the sounds of r in *red, round, bring*: the discernible phonic differences between such sounds are due to the modifying influence of the adjacent sounds.

Phonemic Awareness

Phonemic awareness is the ability to recognize that a spoken word consists of individual sounds in sequence. [The single best predictor of future reading success.]

Phonics

1. The method of teaching reading by training beginners to associate the letter(s) with sound values. 2. The science of sound.

Vowel

A voiced speech sound characterized by generalized friction of the air passing in a continuous stream through the pharynx and open mouth, with relatively no narrowing or other obstruction of the speech organs. A letter, as *a, e, i, o,* and *u,* representing such a sound. distinguished from consonant.

Bibliography

BRYANT, MARGARET, Modern English and Its Heritage, The Macmillan Company,New York, 1948, 1962.

CRAWFORD, D.H., Beowolf, Cooper Square Publishers, Inc., New York, 1966.

SABIN, WILLIAM A., The Gregg Reference Manual, Macmillan/McGraw-Hill, New York, 1992.

GROOM, BERNARD, A Short History of English Words, Macmillan & Co., New York, 1962.

MERRIAM-WEBSTER, WEBSTER'S DICTIONARY OF SYNONYMS, G. & C. Merriam Company, Springfield, Massachusetts, 1942.

MILLER, WARDS S., Word Wealth Junior, Holt, Rinehart and Winston, Inc., New York, 1962.

MONROE, MARION AND BERTIE BACKUS, Remedial Reading, Houghton Mifflin Company, New York, 1937.

PEI, MARIO, The Story of the English Language, J.B. Lippincott Company, New York, 1967.

PYLES, THOMAS, The Origins and Development of the English Language, Harcourt, Brace & World, Inc., New York 1964.

ROBERT, CLYDE, Teacher's Guide to Work Attack, Harcourt, Brace & World, Inc., New York 1956.

READER'S DIGEST, Complete Wordfinder, The Reader's Digest Association, Inc., Pleasantville, New York, 1996.

TAYLOR, ALBERT, JOHN C. GILMARTIN, WILLIAM A. BOYLAN, Correct Spelling with Dictionary Study/ 5th Year, Noble & Noble, Publishers, Inc., New York, New York, 1941.

WEBSTER'S NEW TWENTIETH CENTURY DICTIONARY, 2nd Edition with Outline History of the English Language, unknown publication information.

WOOD, CLEMENT, The Complete Rhyming Dictionary and Poet's Craft Book, Garden City Books, Garden City, New York, 1936.

SPECIAL ACKNOWLEDGEMENT
To George O. Cureton and Jeannie Eller, www.actionreading.com

INDEX
FOR CHAPTER TWO

EDU-STEPS, INC.

~ ~ ~

Dear Reader,

We are pleased to hear from the teachers, parents, and self-learners who say that they enjoy using the materials from Edu-Steps, Inc.

If you have a suggestion, a comment, a question, or a testimony about your successes, please feel free to contact us at www.edu-steps.com. We look forward to hearing from you. Also, if you find this program helpful, please tell others about it. It is available in various media formats.

If you send us a testimony and would permit us to use it on our website and in our advertising materials, please add a note saying that you give us your permission. We will be pleased to use your name or keep your comments anonymous.

Thank you.
--Pat Doran, M.Ed. and Edu-Steps' Team
www.edu-steps.com

Phonics Steps
To
Reading Success

SPELLING JOURNAL

Name_____

_____

© 2008 Edu-Steps, Inc.

This section may be duplicated by purchaser of Phonics Steps to Reading Success Program.
www.edu-steps.com

For Instructor:
1. You do not need to use all lines allotted for each page.
2. Students should self correct.
3. Correct and analyze errors.

Student Tips For Good Handwriting:
1. Write all letters **on** the line.
2. Write all tall letters the same height.
3. Write all small letters the same height.
4. Write all letters straight up and down (||||) or write with a slant using the same slant for all letters (////).
   Do not mix slants. (/|\/\|\/)

CHAPTER ONE

Rule: (Optional)

_____

_____

_____

_____

_____

_____

_____

1. _____
2. _____
3. _____
4. _____
5. _____

Number correct_____

~~~~~~~~~~~~~~~~~~~~~~~~~~~~~~

CHAPTER TWO

Page 1

Rule: (Optional)

_____

_____

_____

_____

_____

_____

1. _____
2. _____
3. _____
4. _____
5. _____
6. _____
7. _____
8. _____
9. _____
10. _____

Number correct_____

~~~~~~~~~~~~~~~~~~~~~~~~~~~~~~

Page 2

Rule: (Optional)

_____

_____

_____

_____

_____

_____

1. _____
2. _____
3. _____
4. _____
5. _____
6. _____
7. _____
8. _____
9. _____
10. _____

Number correct_____

(No spelling quiz for Page 3)

Page **4**

Rule: (Optional)

_____
_____
_____
_____
_____

1. _____
2. _____
3. _____
4. _____
5. _____

Number correct_____

Page **5**

Rule: (Optional)

_____
_____
_____
_____
_____

1. _____
2. _____
3. _____
4. _____
5. _____
6. _____
7. _____
8. _____
9. _____
10. _____

Number correct_____

(No spelling quiz for Pages 6, 7.)

Page **8**

Rule: (Optional)

_____

_____

_____

_____

_____

1. _____
2. _____
3. _____
4. _____
5. _____

Number correct_____

Page **9**

Rule: (Optional)

_____

_____

_____

_____

_____

1. _____
2. _____
3. _____

Number correct_____

(No spelling quiz for Pages 10-12)

Page **13**

(Mark the word. Underline the vowel team, cross out the silent vowel, arrows under each letter that is pronounced.)

1. _____

Page **14**

1. _____
2. _____
3. _____
4. _____
5. _____
6. _____
7. _____
8. _____
9. _____
10. _____

Number correct_____

Page **15**

1. _____
2. _____
3. _____
4. _____
5. _____
6. _____
7. _____
8. _____
9. _____
10. _____

Number correct_____

Page **16**

1. _____
2. _____
3. _____
4. _____
5. _____
6. _____
7. _____
8. _____
9. _____
10. _____

*Number correct*_____

Page **18**

1. _____
2. _____
3. _____
4. _____
5. _____
6. _____
7. _____
8. _____
9. _____
10. _____

*Number correct*_____

Page **17**

1. _____
2. _____
3. _____
4. _____
5. _____
6. _____
7. _____
8. _____
9. _____
10. _____

*Number correct*_____

Page **19**

1. _____
2. _____
3. _____
4. _____
5. _____
6. _____
7. _____
8. _____
9. _____
10. _____

*Number correct*_____

Page **20**

1. _____
2. _____
3. _____
4. _____
5. _____
6. _____
7. _____
8. _____
9. _____
10. _____

Number correct_____

Page **21**

1. _____
2. _____
3. _____
4. _____
5. _____
6. _____
7. _____
8. _____
9. _____
10. _____

Number correct_____

Page **22**

1. _____

2. _____
3. _____
4. _____
5. _____
6. _____
7. _____
8. _____
9. _____
10. _____

Number correct_____

Page **23**

1. _____
2. _____
3. _____
4. _____
5. _____
6. _____
7. _____
8. _____
9. _____
10. _____

Number correct_____

Page **24**

1. _____
2. _____
3. _____
4. _____

5. _____
6. _____
7. _____
8. _____
9. _____
10. _____

Number correct_____

Page **25**

1. _____
2. _____
3. _____
4. _____
5. _____
6. _____
7. _____
8. _____
9. _____
10. _____

Number correct_____

Page **26**

1. _____
2. _____

Number correct_____

Page **27**

1. _____
2. _____
3. _____
4. _____
5. _____
6. _____
7. _____
8. _____
9. _____
10. _____

Number correct_____

Page **28**

1. _____
2. _____
3. _____
4. _____
6. _____

Number correct_____

Page **29**

1. _____
2. _____
3. _____
4. _____
5. _____

6. _____

7. _____

8. _____

9. _____

10. _____

Number correct_____

Page **30**

1. _____

2. _____

3. _____

4. _____

5. _____

6. _____

7. _____

8. _____

Number correct_____

Page **31**

1. _____

2. _____

3. _____

4. _____

5. _____

6. _____

7. _____

8. _____

Number correct_____

(No spelling quiz for Page 32)

Page 33

(Write the word, *bread.* Cross out silent vowel.)

1. _____

Page **34**

1. _____

2. _____

3. _____

4. _____

5. _____

Number correct_____

(No spelling quiz for Page 35.)

Page **36**

1. _____

2. _____

3. _____

4. _____

5. _____

6. _____

7. _____

8. _____

9. _____

10. _____

Number correct_____

Page **37**

1. _____
2. _____
3. _____
4. _____
5. _____
6. _____
7. _____
8. _____
9. _____
10. _____

Number correct_____

Page **38**

Sentence Dictation

1._____

_____

_____

_____

_____

2._____

_____

_____

_____

_____

Page **39**

1. _____
2. _____
3. _____
4. _____
5. _____
6. _____
7. _____
8. _____
9. _____
10. _____

Number correct_____

Page **40**

1. _____
2. _____
3. _____
4. _____
5. _____
6. _____
7. _____
8. _____
9. _____
10. _____

Number correct_____

Page **41**

1. _____
2. _____
3. _____
4. _____
5. _____
6. _____
7. _____
8. _____
9. _____
10. _____

Number correct_____

Page **42**

1. _____
2. _____
3. _____
4. _____
5. _____
6. _____
7. _____
8. _____
9. _____
10. _____

Number correct_____

Page **43**

1. _____
2. _____
3. _____
4. _____
5. _____
6. _____
7. _____
8. _____
9. _____
10. _____

Number correct_____

Page **44**

1. _____
2. _____
3. _____
4. _____
5. _____
6. _____
7. _____
8. _____
9. _____
10. _____

Number correct_____

Page **45**

1. _____
2. _____
3. _____
4. _____
5. _____
6. _____
7. _____
8. _____
9. _____
10. _____

Number correct_____

Page **47**

1. _____
2. _____
3. _____
4. _____
5. _____
6. _____
7. _____
8. _____
9. _____
10. _____

Number correct_____

Page **46**

1. _____
2. _____
3. _____
4. _____
5. _____
6. _____
7. _____
8. _____
9. _____
10. _____

Number correct_____

Page **48**

1. _____
2. _____
3. _____
4. _____
5. _____
6. _____
7. _____
8. _____
9. _____
10. _____

Number correct_____

Page **49**

1. _____
2. _____
3. _____
4. _____
5. _____
6. _____
7. _____
8. _____
9. _____
10. _____

Number correct_____

Page **50**

1. _____
2. _____
3. _____
4. _____
5. _____
6. _____
7. _____
8. _____
9. _____
10. _____

Number correct_____

Page **51**

1. _____

2. _____
3. _____
4. _____
5. _____
6. _____
7. _____
8. _____
9. _____
10. _____

Number correct_____

Page **52**

Sentence Dictation

1._____
_____
_____
_____
_____

2._____
_____
_____
_____
_____

Page **53**

1. _____
2. _____
3. _____
4. _____

5. _____
6. _____
7. _____
8. _____
9. _____
10. _____

Number correct_____

~~~~~~~~~~~~~~~~~~~~~~~~~~~

Page **54**

1. _____
2. _____
3. _____
4. _____
5. _____
6. _____
7. _____
8. _____
9. _____
10. _____

Number correct_____

~~~~~~~~~~~~~~~~~~~~~~~~~~~

(No spelling quiz for Page 55.)

~~~~~~~~~~~~~~~~~~~~~~~~~~~

Page **56**

1. _____
2. _____
3. _____
4. _____

5. _____
6. _____
7. _____
8. _____
9. _____
10. _____

Number correct_____

~~~~~~~~~~~~~~~~~~~~~~~~~~~

Page **57**

1. _____
2. _____
3. _____
4. _____
5. _____
6. _____
7. _____
8. _____
9. _____
10. _____

Number correct_____

~~~~~~~~~~~~~~~~~~~~~~~~~~~

Page **58**

1. _____
2. _____
3. _____
4. _____
5. _____
6. _____
7. _____

8. _____
9. _____
10. _____

*Number correct*_____

8. _____
9. _____
10. _____

*Number correct*_____

Page **59**

1. _____
2. _____
3. _____
4. _____
5. _____
6. _____
7. _____
8. _____
9. _____
10. _____

*Number correct*_____

Page **61**

1. _____
2. _____
3. _____
4. _____
5. _____
6. _____
7. _____
8. _____
9. _____
10. _____

*Number correct*_____

Page **60**

1. _____
2. _____
3. _____
4. _____
5. _____
6. _____
7. _____

Page **62**

1. _____
2. _____
3. _____
4. _____
5. _____

*Number correct*_____

Sentence Dictation

_____

_____

_____

_____

_____

Page **63** and **64**

1. _____
2. _____
3. _____
4. _____
5. _____
6. _____
7. _____
8. _____
9. _____
10. _____

*Number correct*_____

Page **65**

1. _____
2. _____
3. _____
4. _____
5. _____
6. _____
7. _____
8. _____

9. _____
10. _____

*Number correct*_____

(No spelling quiz for Page 66-67.)

Page **68**

1. _____
2. _____
3. _____
4. _____
5. _____
6. _____
7. _____
8. _____
9. _____
10. _____

*Number correct*_____

Page **69** and **70**

1. _____
2. _____
3. _____
4. _____
5. _____
6. _____
7. _____
8. _____

9. _____
10. _____

Number correct_____

Page **71**

1. _____
2. _____
3. _____
4. _____
5. _____
6. _____
7. _____
8. _____
9. _____
10. _____

Number correct_____

Page **72**

1. _____
2. _____
3. _____
4. _____
5. _____
6. _____
7. _____
8. _____
9. _____
10. _____

Number correct_____

Page **73**

1. _____
2. _____
3. _____
4. _____
5. _____
6. _____
7. _____
8. _____
9. _____
10. _____

Number correct_____

Page **74**

1. _____
2. _____
3. _____
4. _____
5. _____
6. _____
7. _____
8. _____
9. _____
10. _____

Number correct_____

Page **75**

1. _____
2. _____
3. _____
4. _____
5. _____
6. _____
7. _____
8. _____
9. _____
10. _____

*Number correct*_____

(No spelling quiz for Page 76.)

Page **77**

1. _____
2. _____
3. _____
4. _____
5. _____
6. _____
7. _____
8. _____
9. _____
10. _____

*Number correct*_____

Page **78**

1. _____
2. _____
3. _____
4. _____
5. _____
6. _____
7. _____
8. _____
9. _____
10. _____

*Number correct*_____

Page **79**

1. _____
2. _____
3. _____
4. _____
5. _____
6. _____
7. _____
8. _____
9. _____
10. _____

*Number correct*_____

(No spelling quiz for Page 80.)

Page **81**

1. _____
2. _____
3. _____
4. _____
5. _____
6. _____
7. _____
8. _____
9. _____
10. _____

Number correct_____

Page **82**

Write the missing words.

1. a._____*insisted*_____
   b._____
2. a. _____
   b. _____
3. a. _____
   b. _____
4. a._____
   b. _____

Number correct_____

Page **83**

1. _____
2. _____
3. _____

4. _____
5. _____
6. _____
7. _____
8. _____
9. _____
10. _____

Number correct_____

Page **83A**

Find the misspelled word
in each sentence.

1. _____
2. _____
3. _____
4. _____
4. _____

Number correct_____

Page **86**

ab-

ab- *means* _____

1. _____
2. _____
3. _____
4. _____
5. _____

Number correct_____

Page **86**
ad-

ad- means _____

1. _____
2. _____
3. _____
4. _____
5. _____

Number correct_____

~~~~~~~~~~~~~~~~~~~~~~~~~~~~

Page **87**
ante-

ante- means _____

1. _____
2. _____
3. _____
4. _____
5. _____

Number correct_____

~~~~~~~~~~~~~~~~~~~~~~~~~~~~

Page **86**
anti-

anti- means _____

1. _____
2. _____

3. _____
4. _____
5. _____

Number correct_____

~~~~~~~~~~~~~~~~~~~~~~~~~~~~

Page **88**
circum-

circum- means _____

1. _____
2. _____
3. _____
4. _____
5. _____

Number correct_____

~~~~~~~~~~~~~~~~~~~~~~~~~~~~

Page **89**
con-

con- means _____

_____

1. _____
2. _____
3. _____
4. _____
5. _____

Number correct_____

Page **89**

contra-

contra – *means* _____

1. _____
2. _____
3. _____
4. _____

*Number correct*_____

Page **90**

de-

de- *means* _____

_____

1. _____
2. _____
3. _____
4. _____
5. _____

*Number correct*_____

Page **90**

dis-

dis- *means* _____

1. _____
2. _____

3. _____
4. _____
5. _____

*Number correct*_____

Page **91**

ex-

ex- *means* _____

_____

1. _____
2. _____
3. _____
4. _____
5. _____

*Number correct*_____

Page **91**

in-

in- *means* _____

1. _____
2. _____
3. _____
4. _____
5. _____

*Number correct*_____

Page **92**
in- ,il-, im-, ir-

In-, il-, im-, ir- means ____
_____

1. _____
2. _____
3. _____
4. _____
5. _____

_Number correct_____

Page **93**
inter-

inter- **means** _____
_____

1. _____
2. _____
3. _____
4. _____
5. _____

_Number correct_____

Page **93**
intra-/intro-

intra- means _____

1. _____

2. _____
3. _____
4. _____
5. _____

_Number correct_____

Page **94**
mis-

mis- means _____
1. _____
2. _____
3. _____
4. _____
5. _____

_Number correct_____

Page **95**
per-

per- means _____

1. _____
2. _____
3. _____
4. _____
6. _____

_Number correct_____

Page **96**
pre-

pre- means _____

1. _____
2. _____
3. _____
4. _____
5. _____

Number correct_____

~~~~~~~~~~~~~~~~~~~~~~~~~~~~~~~

Page **96**
post-

post- means _____

1. _____
2. _____
3. _____
4. _____
5. _____

Number correct_____

~~~~~~~~~~~~~~~~~~~~~~~~~~~~~~~

Page **97**
pro-

pro- means _____

1. _____
2. _____
3. _____
4. _____

5. _____

Number correct_____

~~~~~~~~~~~~~~~~~~~~~~~~~~~~~~~

Page **98**
re-

re- means _____

1. _____
2. _____

3. _____
4. _____
5. _____

Number correct_____

~~~~~~~~~~~~~~~~~~~~~~~~~~~~~~~

Page **99**
se-

se- means _____

1. _____
2. _____
3. _____
4. _____
5. _____

Number correct_____

~~~~~~~~~~~~~~~~~~~~~~~~~~~~~~~

Page **99**
sub-

sub- means _____

1. _____
2. _____
3. _____
4. _____
5. _____

Number correct_____

Page **100**
super-

super- means _____

1. _____
2. _____
3. _____
4. _____
5. _____

Number correct_____

Page **100**
trans-

trans- means _____

1. _____
2. _____
3. _____
4. _____
5. _____

Number correct_____

Page **101**
un-

un- means _____

1. _____
2. _____
3. _____
4. _____
5. _____

Number correct_____

Page **101**
uni-

uni- means _____

1. _____
2. _____
3. _____
4. _____
5. _____

Number correct_____

Page **101**
bi-

bi- means _____

1. _____
2. _____

3. _____
4. _____
5. _____

*Number correct*_____

Page **101**

tri-

tri- *means* _____

1. _____
2. _____
3. _____
4. _____
5. _____

*Number correct*_____

Page **102**
(Numbers 1-10)

1. _____
2. _____
3. _____
4. _____
5. _____
6. _____
7. _____
8. _____
9. _____
10. _____

*Number correct*_____

Page **102**
(Numbers 11-18)

11. _____
12. _____
13. _____
14. _____
15. _____
16. _____
17. _____
18. _____

Number correct_____

Page **103**

Rule: _____

_____

_____

_____

1. _____
2. _____
3. _____
4. _____
5. _____

Sentence Dictation

_____

_____

_____

_____

_____

*Y*ou *have almost completed the program. We saved the most confusing for last! If you worked hard, this should be a pi*ē*ce of cake!*

Page **104**

1. _____
2. _____
3. _____
4. _____
5. _____
6. _____
7. _____
8. _____
9. _____
10. _____

Number correct_____

◆ ◆ ◆

CONGRATULATIONS!!

You have completed the
Phonics Steps to Reading Success' Spelling Journal!

Always strive to spell correctly.

Pay attention to spelling troublemakers and vowel teams when you read. If you do, it will be easier to spell correctly when you write.

You will be proud and glad that you are a good speller.

You will do well!